An Edwardi
in Lon

CW00860451

Donald C Naismith

ISBN:1492995363
ISBN-13:9781492995364

DEDICATED

To

Grandad

Ernest Edward Jennings
1901-1979

Forward

In January 1975 an elderly man sat down at his equally old writing desk and began composing a letter to his daughter, Joyce. One would think that there was nothing special in this event, as hundreds of parents write to their children every day. However, this letter was just the first one in a series that proved to be special in a very unique way and the story that they told is truly remarkable.

Ernest Edward Jennings was a very private man, proud, hard working and very capable. He also had a lot of 'Mick' in him, hot headed with a short fuse, not someone you would want to get on the wrong side of. His previous letters to his daughter Joyce were always lengthy and detailed, showing his love of writing, a skill he only mastered in his early twenties as a young man in the army. This particular series of letters was prompted by a casual remark by his daughter that she knew nothing of his childhood or early adulthood. Neither Joyce nor any of her siblings(i) had any knowledge of their father's upbringing for he had never spoken of it.

To the casual reader the story contained in this book will give a fascinating insight into the ordinary lives of those living and working in the shadow of poverty in the early 20th century. The deprivation suffered by millions in the city that was the very hub of the British Empire is brought to life within these pages. To the student of the Edwardian era, the detailed description of institutions and practices which existed to deal with the problem of the poor, will bring the subject to life.

Perhaps it was the realisation of his own mortality that prompted him to begin, and once begun it was as though a dam had burst. What followed was a series of letters detailing his life from his earliest memories to early adulthood, and gives a very real insight into life in the early years of the 20th century.

I have endeavoured to faithfully transcribe his letters, neither adding to nor omitting anything that he had written. I have, where I have considered necessary, added explanatory notes which may be found in the notes at the end of this book.

(i) See Note 1

Prelude

January 14th 1975

HULLO! And it is a 'cheery one' – on this occasion; because your short and sweet letter of the 12th inst. has set the mood for the following pages, and the sentence viz. "Early Childhood Memories" "would I like to try my hand at that…'' of course, of course, of course – for nothing ventured, nothing done:

I shall be entirely at my ease in 'wrapping round' your subject with a pleasure, providing of course: - you make allowances at my age and ability to retrace back over some 69 years of events. Time will maybe tend to blur some of the kaleidoscopic pictures of my childhood as I try to recall them to mind and in receding back for just an half a decade –from 1912 to 1906- I will bring back to light some of the best of prominent highlights of those formative years. I specify 1912 – being then just eleven years of age, and 1912 was to determine my future years of, shall I say, Adventure into life proper'.

To commence prior to 1906 will give you, the reader, a conceptive (sic) view of my background environment of those tender years from out of their mists. I have only scraps of recollection and will not in any way interfere with my memories of later years. They are just a prelude to my factual recollections.

On Friday the 13th of September 1901, there was born at no. 27 Croydon Road, Plaistow, London E13, a son to George Frederick William and Mary Ann Jennings. If there were any jubilation over this event I am not aware of it. There had been 15 of them before my arrival and I can genealogically name 12 of them, who Ernest Edward became the 13th of the then living members of the ''Tribe of Jenningses'' as we were known.

Family births in those Victoriana and Edwardian days was a 'gala occasion' bringing the collection of relatives and Uncles-Aunts and Cousins and neo 'In Laws'. It was an excuse to bury the hatchet of past tribal clashes and warfare- who all came 'in Pack' to view the latest additive arrival, and to be sure a definite call for a Welsh-Irish booze up. Which I dare say ended up with a wee scrap and a visit to the local court for judicial scrutiny.

Records will show my Fathers side was of the
sea going class and a right old hard class they were
in the 17th 18th 19th and 20th centuries. Mothers side
were of blue-blooded inhabitants of Irish Corkians,
hard as nails and intensive of purpose and never
could nor would 'Lower the Flag' to a dare! Nor
would avoid a challenge if someone (my how I pity
them) ever lowered the boom to her and -the
strange part of ancestry- Grand dad and Grand
mamma were of the same extraction. So in it is
truly – 'Two parts Iroish (sic) and 1 part Welsh
(Glamorganshire if that counts for anything?) in my
makeup. The Welsh are not Jibbos either when a
point of prestige is at stake, and it was into this
environment –of the days of <u>BIG</u> families in which
'one more of less' didn't alter things much and
counted as just one more mouth to feed and was
taken into the stride of things. Mum was fourtyish
–change of life period- when I was conceived and I
was to be the last (bless him), and the last I was, I
dare say.

I was kissed, cuddled and fussed over on that
occasion (who knows?) but since then –ah ha- I
was to receive more cuffs than 'appiness. Since
then it transpired that Grand dad and Grand mama
tried to dampen any exuberant feelings by saying:
(1) I was a Jonah
(2) Born on Friday the 13th
(3) I would meet troubled tides because:
(4) I was a chip off the old block,

(Of which remark I can only assume emanating from Grand dad's experiences of the said George Frederick William other sons).

Uncles 'Stormy' 'Masty' Arthur, John and Horatio (Tom) a rare boyo in his cups! I was to know each one, and to each I was the proverbial 'Mick' of the male side. On the religious side of life I was brought up under non-conformist tuition. The Bible was the No1 book of their lives, at sea and on land and I was taught of a strict rule (and plenty of leather belt) never to impinge nor traverse the ways of the ungodly. I was never allowed to forget it.

As I have stated I have only mists of recollections of those early days. As rough and tough as they were in their every day ways, they were a generous, kind collection of men to me. I was the baby and as such, lavished love upon. Grand dad took me under his wing with his advisory to Dad –"Ill make something of him for you, Mary and George" -. I was to spend my early days with him and Grand mama. Apparently I was the most inquisitive -always up to some caper or other- child that they had ever known. "You don't have to show or tell him twice George, he's got it!" I can remember his beard, like Dads, an Imperial Edwardian one which used to tickle me as he kissed me, which was quite often, and the fringe of his moustache was tinged by the beer he drank, 'grog' he called it. "But none for little boys to drink!" I can still recall his hot 'coffee and rum' breathing. I can recall when Auntie Emily died Grand dad and his sons, 6 in number, split a flagon of pure Jamaican rum in one session after the funeral. The air reeked with it, and to top it off had a keg of xxx (3x) beer in the parlour where a few hours previous Auntie Em had lain to be screwed and battened down. Time came for me to be put to bed and in the bedroom over the parlour I could hear voices raised – Dad started to play his Concertina. Mum coming up to see we were alright, and uncles Stormy and Masty coming to the bedside to see, as they termed one, your Cockalorum Mary! Uncle Stormy saying "You be a good boy to mummy and you shall have the Polly Parrot Mick". ((Do you) recall that same parrot Joy that I took to our Ron?) When Uncle Stormy died in 1939, just after the war broke out I went to Poplar to collect it. Mick had got his parrot after all those years; some 34 years after the above took place (Which gives you marker date of the age period of when it took place…).

To arrive at a starting point of recollections I will start at 1909 and work back in my "Story/Essay", back in retrospect to the fringe of the "mists". Uncle Stormy was in his 80th year then. What a man, what a pal! I leave them to rest in peace to face their 'Ship Master'.

My Dad was 40ish when he died in 1911, after a long illness of 18 months resulting from a fall down a ships hold –SS Carpentaria-(i) of the New Zealand Shipping Company at the dry dock of Lester Perkins Albert Dock, Silvertown E16.

As I have stated, I'll commence my memoirs from my 11th birthday in 1912, which being in the first decade of an adventurous life I can only truly trace 6 to 20 years with true accuracy… I will add nothing superlative nor deduct any episode which I can clearly recall with authenticity. The years from 1912 to 1909 are clearly stamped on my mind. The years 1912 onwards to 1974 are only too easy to recall. My 11th birthday commencing my arrival at the gates of the Workhouse in Leytonstone Road(ii) remain one of the most miserablist (sic) days and nights of my life, which was to bring out the "Mick" out in me.

(i)   See Note 2
(ii)   See Note 3

Chapter One

Subject: Early Childhood Memories circa 1906-1912...

Dear Reader

If I am to follow J B Priestley's advice that in writing a story one must get to the point in the least possible words, I have then to curtail, out of necessity, a lot of superficial details. To make a complete story in all its detail would necessitate my having a tape or Dictaphone recorder by my side, an audio stenographer and type writer as the small details are recalled, record them at leisure. I cannot afford to possess these essentials so you, the reader, will have to contend and progress the best way you can, to decipher my wretched writing. The old hand is getting shaky now, eyes are becoming dim, and the urge to get this story to paper is keen. My mind is still, thank goodness, sharp with the animal sharpness which one would see in a dog or a cat or wild animal, upon which it depends for its very existence. Allow this to be

(1) Heredital (sic)
(2) Grand dads training

(3) A varied life in the formative years

(4) Sea life in the teen age years

(5) The service training in young adult life

(6) The civilian life afterwards

(7) The acceptance of circumstantial events up to retirement age

(8) Culminating in brining to bear and being all past experiences into motive design to overcome the deadly innuendo of living alone in silence. (Not 'lonely' you will note, I am too occupative (sic) to be that).

Because, as Grand dad was wont to teach, "Son, there will be lonely hours at the wheel house of quietness, when all you will hear is the singing of the wind up in the shrouds. She will sing to you, you will not be lonely, listen to her, but keep you mind and eyes on you compass bearing. Fix your point, take your soundings and stay alert. Never allow the quietness lull you to nod off in sleep. Other lives depend upon you as you will depend on them when you are off watch!! Keep reason as your mother and you will not go adrift".

I ask you reader; be patient with me in my writings and although I may be old I can still have young ideas of my "Childhood memories". I am still able mentally to relive them even though the spring and alacrity of movement may have left my body.

Before I commence my retrospect of my days of Childhood I would want to add a Prefix to tell the reader that the writer is a septuagenarian whose childhood days were spent in the Post Victorian/Edwardian days, those days of "Children should be seen and not heard". When the social amenities were so different from these "Security from want".

There are no poor people today; there is no Workhouse – the Lump as it was called. There are no Bailiffs to walk into the home, there are no Pubs opened all day from 5AM 'till midnight. There are no 3 Brass Balls, which signified the Pop (pawnshop) where Dads suit could be put in to pay the rent. There are no 'apporths and pennorths' today, when one could spend 4 1/2 pence and buy enough vegetables and choice 'scrag' a bit of suet, a half pound bag of flour, a pennorth of currents and raisins a penny in the gas (a new innovation in 1906) and make a 'Duff' big enough to fill five empty tummies... A housewife was indeed fortunate to have 12/- to 14/- per week to feed a family of from 5-16. A working man was indeed well off to earn 25/- a week (Rent 6/6 to 8/-). For this sum his working week would be 72 hours without any security of 'established going to work' on any given day.

It was a different world of those days, living in the East End of London, in the days of Horse

Trams and street hawkers, crying their wares. When one would see six policemen and a sergeant walk in pairs in the gutter, being smartly marched to their 'Beat'. A policeman in those days was a person to be respected. So see a Bobbie at some ones door would mean curtains being peered through and occasion for a choice morsel of gossip! The shops were stocked with all descriptions of food and the odd farthing was a purchasable valued coin. One never saw 'it' marked up – it was 11 3/4d and to own, as a child, a whole farthing, to spend once a week, why! My goodness, your parents had to be rich and well off. To have a 'New Penny' at Christmas in your stocking sent one up to the highest of heavens.

It would take me a long time of many words and pages to describe my childhood days of that Edwardian Era. It lasted just for a decade, half of which, to the age of 5 years, from 1901 to 1906, only certain outstanding highlights come to mind. My preceding writing of this period is outlined on pages 4-7. I start my recollections from 1906 and relate from incidents from that year onwards, till 1912. I shall endeavour to write a clear, concise digest of those years. Even then keep my tongue in my cheek because I do not wish to confuse any reader by adding superlatives, confectual (sic) or otherwise, but just plain memories of these highlights which were to end in tragedy, pathos and culminating in distress for me.

The problem of writing an essay on 'Childhood Days' is how to condense into as few words and sentences of some 1,725 days, each having their own content, to weave an outstanding and lucid picture to convey to the reader. Portraying an era of time that is totally different of some 60 years afterwards.

I seem to want atmosphere to help me commence, so, to get into the mood of retrospection I shall hum a suitable tune of 'The Gay Twenties' called:

Memories, memories, dreams of long ago
O'er the sea of memories, Im drifting back to you
Childhood days, wildhood ways among the bugs and fleas
Now Im alone and here on my own
I sit with my beautiful memories

Christmas 1905/6, I recollect its highlights, lying awake, waiting to hear the 'Waite' (sic) when the carol singers, with a lighted candle in a lamp upon a pole, stood underneath the street gas lamp (which was situated outside our front door). I was even allowed (shhhhhh!) to creep out of my bed to look wonder eyed at them, wrapped in scarf, mufflers, singing lustily: Good King Wenceslas – Christmas Awake Salute the Happy Morn. The

music was a concertina and cymbals', how so
entrancing it was. A "Quick now – back into bed"
and the words "And Father Christmas will soon be
here so go to sleep, now, or he will not come down
the chimney if he knows you are awake!"

The stockings of my sister Kitty, my brother
Horace and my own were hanging on the bed rail,
seeming like lonely sentinels. Snuggled up warm
we three were soon fast asleep. The morning came;
sleepy eyes open to perceive that 'Father
Christmas' had truly been, for there were bulging
stockings abaft the stern! A scramble took place,
each to their own; a rapid search soon divulged the
cargo… A box of paints, a book of different
drawings, a box of crayons, a bag of pearl drops, an
orange, an apple, a bag of chocolate money and a
real brand new 1906 bright penny. Each one of we
three had the same except Kitty, who had a box of
needlework in lieu of paints; such treasure to have
as ones own. Mum came in and kissed us (with a
special hug for me) saying "good morning Kitty,
Horace, Ernest, Merry Christmas dears!"
To which we duly answered "Good morning dear
Mama. Happy Christmas".

I remember this Christmas very plainly,
because I was allowed home. I was being looked
after by Grand dad and Grand mama at their house.
I was being 'brought up' conforming to the
atmosphere of the sea. I never ever slept in a bed,

but had my own hammock in my 'cabin' (a tiny back room upstairs). Frugal in contents, a sea chest was my wardrobe – to sit on – my various 'toys' were models of ships and boats, a bit of spun yarn hemp, a brad and splicing tool, bits of oak or teak, bits of linen canvas, a pair of scissors, needles, palm pad, a net needle (which I was made to make for myself. Always under the twinkling discerning eyes of Grand dad. He would spend his life with me, always kind, always patient, guiding, instructing and teaching me in my tender years the craft of being a sailor and merry were the days we spent. Grand mama, a kind and goodly soul to me, but to her I was always 'Ernest, a broth of a bhoy!' (How so the memory is).

Grand dad would say "Fish bloater tea son – eh?" and "there is no taste like a bloater cooked on the grid iron of a Kitchener stove", no tea tastes like a five minute simmer on the stove, the real Irish may to make tea. No bread ever tasted like Grand mamas, no toast with its pork dripping lavishly spread upon it. Piles of Rokker Skate with parsley sauce, which clung to the touch, no sprats, dipped in flour to be eaten bones and all and regularly, twice a week, a slab of Salt Cod to fill you up! Ships jam on roly-poly, suety Duff, black treacle and molasses and flap jacks and lots of 'Spuds and Bubble and Squeak with red cabbage. He used to say "You cannot fight and sail on tripe and custard". So, my Christmas spent in a bed was very strange to me but I was yet to sleep in stranger places!

Girls in those days had long plaits of hair, each plait with a very dainty ribbond bow. A pretty frilled dress which reached to the calves with a pinafore, long black stockings and button up boots which were done up by a deft twist of a hook, and always a wee hanky was pinned to their dress. Their decorum was very lady-like among the lower orders, one would occasionally see a 'Tom Boy' type the sexes were kept strictly apart, girls with girls and boys, in their age groups, played with boys. Children of my age group were deemed to be too young to partake in the horseplay and high jinx – Kracker (charging) tug o war. We could play marbles, picture blank with cigarette cards on the window sills or 'skate' them (the cards) to the wall using spans (the span of our small hands) to decide the winner, he whose card was closest to the wall. The strict instructions to play in a given area "Where we can keep an eye on you" and outside this area was taboo, you ventured at your own risk and many a scrap yours truly had over breaking this embargo! I'd take 'em on, big or the same size and Mick was a loner most of the time, the 'Odd man out'. Horace and I were always having a knuckle as he tried to 'Older brother' boss me! So, we were best apart!

Boys average dress code was Haircut, short back and sides neatly sleeked down into a parting where lice were found – a' Convict ' 00 was often seen. Eton collar, washable stiff linen, a bow black 'Pee Pot' cap set on the head was the order and when addressing an elder the boy would take it off to show respect. A belted jacket, short trews or knick bockers and long stockings to reach the knee with laced up boots and that was him dressed.

The jacket pockets contained a varied assortment of odds and ends, but again, a strict 'No hands in the trews pockets and no slovenness. We were allowed to play out till dusk and we youngsters 'till 5 in the summer and never in the early dark nights of winter. It was, living with Grand dad, that I learned to live on my own, finding my own amusements. That I became a loner which was to stand me in good stead in latter years.

Tonight I shall write of a 'Usual Saturday' in childhood, from the age of six, pinpointing at least one episode which clearly stands out in my recollection – but of that later. Firstly, I used to love Saturdays, when I came 'home' after living with Grand dad and my Grand mama. I was in a different ship altogether, a different 'Skipper' mate and crew (a pretty kettle o' fish I can assure you). Where, with Grand dad, I was allowed a certain amount of laxity and he could stand 'so much' until his belt came off (which he only had to point to) to get me all 'snug and battened down again, and his 'You'll get your sails reefed down my lad if you do that again' and a cautionary look from Grand mama. I was aboard a Barque whose 'Skipper' (Dad) never gave an order twice and in true sailor fashion I had to repeat any directions to make sure I had my bearings right! It was into this that I was 'Bag and Duffled', and was to know it, with no molly coddling. I landed home on a Saturday preparatory to start my induction to school. I was in time to go with Kitty and Horace with a big sack to the saw mill to get a penny bag of sawdust for the rabbits, which were kept in the back yard. Dad kept rabbits because in them was always fresh food to be had aboard when a meal was needed. Dad, with his short quick chop behind the ears soon ended their career! On the hearth he had a double hook behind the scullery door shaped like a clothes hanger and he would hook up the poor bunny on this and deftly slice its belly open, take out its entrails and allow it to cool. It used to steam as the air cooled these still warm parts, ugh! But it was dinner after all said and done. Dad said 'They're better'n those Australian rabbits', which you could buy for sixpence ha'penny on Tommy England's stall in the Barking Road. 'For at least you know this is a fresh 'un'. We always had twelve rabbits, six bucks and six doe's, they were real beauties and always a source of interest to me. The sawdust duly being carted home and put in the dry greenhouse . Outside of the greenhouse was a flagstaff, sparred like a ships mast from which, on occasions, there would be pennants and flags flown, such as Trafalgar Day for instance, and what a colourful gay sight to see in the breeze. I've been up top, to unfurl any lines and flags that were twisted and snarled in the rigging. I was a dab hand ('a natural George's true monkey boy' Grand dad would say). I could handle the lanyard or halyards with born ease, any 'clues' wanted to be spliced and it was 'Hey Mr. Joker, make fast and secure'. I would repeat his orders, emphasising the 'Mr. Joker' part loud and clear. 'Aye aye sir' and many are the happy Saturday afternoons I have spent being made to repeat 'Top Royal, Top Gallants fore and aft, Main Sail and Mizzen, Fore sheet and Jib sheets 1,2.3'. I could furl a sheet or sail neater than any deck hand and I wasn't yet eight! At the base of the mast was a binnacle and wind vane. I was taught to read this and could recite 'The Box' off pat far quicker than Horace could, which, at least put me one up on him, it became second nature to me. I simply loved it, anything to do with sailing ships still do. I love the smell of oakum and tarred rope; I like the feel of the wool I crochet.

When the sawdust was safely stowed away our dinner was ready. Let me tell you of the dinner which was never altered. We had two means of cooking, the Kitchener stove and the new-fangled gas stove in the back room (kitchen cum general use room). The scullery held the 'sluicing' sink, a big deep ships wooden one, a 'Copper in which all clothes were boil washed on Mondays, being coal or log fired, and a cupboard that held soaps and miscellaneous cleaning tackle which was used in any home of that period. A galley, true ships style, was rigged up by Dad in the kitchen, shelves held copper pots and pans, polished and shining with 'Brickdust' cleaning and rubbing. The choice of cleaning gear was:

(1) Brickdust
(2) Old Dutch Cleanser
(3) Monkey Brand
(4) Wellington Knife Cleaner
(5) Brasso
(6) Whiting

Of these, Brickdust was deemed the best. To clean and polish the Kitchener and fender Zebro was used, a little vinegar added to its shine with lots of elbow grease could make that kitchen gleam (it was mother's pride, next to her curtains and antimacassar's). The top of the fender was of bright steel and upon that stood the grid iron and horseshoe stand, on which stood the tea pot off the hob. There were three kettles, all copper with brass handles and everything looking ship shape and Bristol fashion, it was indeed a picture to look at. (You would have loved it Joy, for, perhaps hereditarily, this is where you got your liking for brass and copper work, who knows?). The kitchen 'galley' was 'abaft the mast' and as such out of bounds to us 'crew' and very rarely were we allowed into it. It was sacrosanct to Mum. Saturdays dinner consisted of sausages, onions, mash potatoes and when in season parsnips and swedes. The sangers (that's the way you used to say it Joy) were pan fried and put to one side, piles of them from the German butchers Schmidt and Co, Bretony. Onions, of which there were strings of them (which all used at sea) and have their own flavour. 'Big Whites' a potato which would keep all the year round and when cooked were balls of flour, easily mashed. A sauce was made of flour (plain) and water to a consistency of runny paste and with the onions fried, were put over the half flame of gas and brought slowly to the bubble point and allowed to simmer for a little while. A tablespoon, specially kept for the job, was filled with brown sugar, held over the flame until it too bubbled and was mixed as a browning into the simmering onions and flour. The sausages were then added to finish off. Plates taken, piping hot from the over, slices of brown bread crisp fried in bacon fat and dinner was ready! Its smell alone was so appetisingly delicious and inviting, in other words, scrumptious and nice. Grace was duly said (and always we were washed and spruced before sitting down), we asked to begin, which was acquiesced too and we had the 'feed of the Gods'. I have never forgotten that lovely dinner ever, nor tasted on compared to it. I love Saturdays. After dinner the usual procedure: we were allotted the task of going up 'Inky Lane' to where the ink works were, to collect knotted grass, which was a supplement to the rabbits diet. We'd linger over this, Kitty keeping tabs on the time by the chimney clock of the nunnery and on filling our bags we would lark about until it was time to go home. When we got home tea would be ready, a bloater or kipper or sprat or a special treat of rokker skate or cod or haddock pieces. The days menu never altered as long as Dad lived, even when he was ill, until he died, it never varied. I believe Grand dad was responsible, for this was a big bloater, cooked on the grid iron. To me it still is my favourite fish in any shape or form and any seen in front of me is soon made short work of.

Saturday night was bath night in the sitting room in the winter, in front of a roaring fire; a big round tub was filled with warm water, carbolic soap and lots of glorious soaking and splashing until we shone rosy red. I loved those moments, put me near water and I was in my element. During summer we were 'tubbed' outside. We cleaned our teeth with carbolic powder, a pinkish slab in a tin and it would burn like billy oh! Let me see if I can recall the name, ah yes, its label trade mark was flames coming out of a dragon's mouth, a ringed dragon and its name was Eucryl. One penny a tin, lasted ages where I was concerned, I detested it and would dodge the issue whenever possible. Carbolic tooth powder, ugh! Liquorice powder was another I hated and every Saturday night I, or we, were given a dollop of this noxious stuff. I'd invariably vomit mine up until a more acceptable laxative was found. Because of my liking for fish I was given cod liver oil at Grand dads suggestion. Good old Grand dad, I'd eat a bucket of it, bless him for that thought. Dad would invariably bring in some pear drops, four ounces for a penny and we would have four each (and save the rest for the week). Up to bed we would go, sucking our pear drop, or we'd have a few acid drops (if a cold developed, some Rowlands Paregoric tablets or Eucalyptus toffee took the place of our usual issue).

I will now give you a story of the Kitchener episode, a story of domestic warfare in No. 27 Croydon Road, so here goes, from an eye witness and every word is true, hand on heart. I cannot pin-Point the exact date but it was a Saturday, we had gone as usual to get the sawdust and I suppose, something had cropped up to cause Mum to delay dishing up dinner for us children. Dads though, was already in the oven keeping warm when in walks Dad, oiled and stoked up to his gills, he reels in and sits down (I am already sitting in my usual corner of the room). Horace and Kitty were stowing the sawdust away. Mum got his dinner out and set it before him, he said to Mum, 'Children had theirs yet Mary?' and Mum replied 'No, not yet George…something, something' My lord, George got up, picked up his dinner plate and flung it at the fireplace, all over Mums beautiful stove, saying

'None for them, none for me!' Mum looked at him
and said 'Now George, you'll clean that lot up, if
you don't I'll rub your nose in it 'till you do'.
Fancy saying that to the Skipper, sheer
unadulterated mutiny! He said 'I'll see you
buggered first before I do it!' then, silly man, he
turned his back on her. By now her 'Paddy' was up
and raring to come out of the cage and go to Dublin
and back. She grabbed him by his collar and arse of
his trousers, turned him as neatly as she would her
big bed and threw him at the fireplace. He hit the
stove jib on and Mum proceeded to carry out her
word and rub his face along the Kitchener front.
Dad screamed and tried to push himself away with
his hand, which started to sizzle, but Mum 'cock-a-
rides' him, astride his back, rub, rub, rub. Poor
George was toasting and screaming. Kitty
screamed too and rushed out and got Mr. Carter to
come in, I was too scared to move. Mr. Carter went
to bowl Mum over off of Dad, mum picked herself
to her feet and hit Mr. Carter so hard he went
through the yard door as if a mule had kicked him.
He scrambled over the fence and away. Somehow,
a short while afterwards two big policemen came
through the passage and shoo'd us children out to
Mr. Van de Leur next door. I was crying, Kitty was
crying, where Horace was I don't know. I know
that Kitty and I slept in Mr. Van de Leus house that
night and weren't allowed out all that Sunday until
Grand dad came and took me back to his place.
Kitty went to Sarah's home. I think Horace went to

Mr. Dora's, though I'm not sure. I know a week went by with no school for me for Mum had set about the coppers and was doing seven days somewhere for it. Dad was wreathed in bandages. I can recall his words to Uncles Stormy and Masty, they were 'Well, I asked for it and I got it! I must have got her Paddy up somehow' and he let it go at that. I stayed at Grand dads until it all blew over. When I saw Mum next time there was a trace of two black eyes on that sweet face, and her lip still swollen, so somewhere along the line she had continued to scrap with someone until subdued. Dad never did throw another dinner in the fireplace of no. 27! That was one Saturday on which I missed a dinner and seem to recollect Dad staying sober, if that means anything, but in that part of London, home fights were a common occurrence, wife bashing a common occurrence. But to see a man who had been put through the mill by his 'Missus' was a rare advent indeed.

I know that it took a contraption called a stretcher to get Mama to the station. This stretcher was a two wheeled hospital stretcher, hooded at one end, made of brown canvas with two inch straps to contain and restrain the body to be taken to the station. Two clips, fore and aft, unlatched, allowing the stretcher with its load to be carried with ease. The hood being raised up as one sees on a pram to stop the public's inquisitive gaze seeing the passenger. I know that Jimmy Hill got a thump from yours truly when he 'Yah ha'd' me saying that he had seen my Mum being tied on the stretcher. His mother made the mistake of complaining to my Mum of what I had done to her poor Jimmy and Mum would have done the same to her but I think Mrs. Hill saw the 'red light' just in time, retreated and so saved her bacon.

The time Mrs. Noel overstepped the mark and 'lowered the boom' on Mum, there was no pulling of hair and the usual scratching of faces. I was a real stand up toe to toe affair. Mum had chalked a line in the middle of the street, put her toe on the line and said 'Now, you load mouthed cow, see if you can put me of that!' And Mrs. Noel just couldn't. But the coppers were called out yet once more and when it quietened down and they left, over to No. 18 went Mum, got Mrs. Noel again and the poor woman got a 'She larruping' a la Irish mode for Mrs. Noel to remember her by. 'Teach her to keep her trap shut or I'll shut it up for her!' Mum wasn't in the habit of making idle promises! Yes, the Jenningses were sort of know thereabouts I can assure you. Grand dad could put in a few words, 'If you want to lower the boom on Mary Ann I caution you to think twice about it. You'll only find she is stuffing it down your throat and ready to follow it too, just to make sure it is safely stowed away' So you see, they were brought up in hard days of very strict rules. If you were not capable of putting you 'dukes' up and defending

27

yourself, to row your own boat, you were well and truly trodden upon. To 'sail before the mast' you ad to be tough, rough and ready, to meet hell and high water come wind and storm. When you signed Ships Articles you took whatever was coming and it wasn't to moan over. To moan was to verge on 'mutiny' and severe were the rule and methods used to stop any shenanigans. It was stamped on then and there and no tolerance allowed. In those days there was no such thing as 'hard luck' if you didn't work, you didn't eat, as simple as that. If, as children, you didn't have toys, you made your own amusements. Toys were a scarcity, a marble, a button, a screw or a fag picture were all jealously owned and guarded. They were a means of trade and barter. A peg top, a bit of string, a cotton reel, a nail, a comic, a pair of skates, a hoop, a skipping rope, a kite, a piece of chalk, bits of make believe china or dolls or colour crepe paper to make a grotto, shells and picture postcards to adorn the said grotto, a whip and top and various other treasures were our means of amusement. As I have said, there were seasons of the year in which different 'toys' were in fashion. An empty Colmans mustard tin with holes punched in the top and bottom stuffed with a rag. You would 'con' some man to light it for you and so make a 'Winter warmer' to keep your hands warm. As you blew onto it the acrid smoke would make your eyes water. Girls had mittens, self made, in rainbow colours and muffs to put their hands in.

Little Eddie Brown, who was a cripple, and I would sit and make table mats of plaited rope , a soda sack, a half a clothes peg and lots of cut up strips of different coloured cloth to make a rug for the front of the fire. We would sit patiently, hour after hour making rugs, I could plait three strands and with my triangle needle and palm pad, make you a door mat you would be proud to own. Give ma a spool of cocoa nut yarn and I'd make you a hammock strong enough to hold a bull, a net to go 'tiddler' fishing with over in the 'swamps'. A true 'loners' way of life, even as a 'bairn' I'd always fall foul of some pugnacious boy and I'd be in hot water again (was I ever out of it?) We Jennings cannot bear to be bossed around and woe to the one who tries it on! As Grand dad was want to say 'We are all tarred with the same brush, easy going until tested!'

The 'Jonah' of the Paddy and Taffy is in all of us and to 'lower the boom' on any of us, then watch out. We cannot stand that! It is this hereditary make up, this trait of character that is prominent in each one of us. Do not, if you want peace, attempt to take this away from us, you would only live to regret it because it is our heritage. The 'We are our own boat and will sail it as we wish' we can be led but not driven. Give us our lee way, grease the spindle of the wheel, load us with enough, just enough, canvas and the elements can have the very devil in them and we'll continue to sail easy like. Sweet childhood memories, what stories I could write about. Seventy years can be a long span, but as I write these words I am 5,6 and 7 years of age all over again. It is easy for me because the memories have stayed put in the 'cargo hold' of a sturdy well built ship. Nurtured into shape by a Ship Wright and Master in the shape of my Grand dad. In an effort to emulate him I have even grown a beard like him and developed his nature of seeing a lesson in everything, retaining a sense of humour and being able to laugh at adversity.

Christmas morning, tip toeing quietly down stairs to have a 'sluice' under the cold water tap. Sissy Horace wanted warm water to wash in. Our first scrap of the day, for he ha commandeered the towel so I belted him one and wiped myself on my shirt. We had an Oatmeal porridge breakfast and wiped a slice of bread round the bacon pan (at least I did!), washed down with a mug of tea, sweetened with Nestles or 'Goats' brand condensed milk and molasses sugar. It always made the tea look like coffee and taste like cocoa!

We each cleared out own things, Mugs and plates away and after, saying grace (remember that routine Joy?) and thanking mummy for a nice breakfast. One to wash up, one to wipe up and one to put away and then seeing everything 'ship shape and Bristol fashion, returned quietly to sit down and play with our new toys! Mum busily preparing inner, the Kitcher stove stoking up a steady 'On the blood' heat. Kitty was 9 years of age and able to help Mum. Horace had to feed the rabbits, which were outside in their hutches, with a mixture of bran, oats and cut up bread. He then had to clean out and re-sawdust the hutches.

We were to have dinner in the parlour and Dad had got the fire blazing merrily. Of the 'sacrosanct' rooms in the house the Parlour, parent's bedroom and dads little 'cabin' were places taboo – out of bounds to ever enter. There was a dividing double door, which could make the Parlour and sitting room into one. Dad, to keep his eye on Mr Joker, Mick, invited me to join him and I went into there, the holy of holies with a marked deference of awe and wonderment! They were gaily decorated with chains and bells, holly and mistletoe. Big laurel leaves and coloured plaques on the walls, and, on the table in the corner were bowls of nuts, figs, dates, oranges and apples. A box of confits which all looked very tempting, exciting and inducive (if only to touch?). The odour of dinner cooking was prevalent. My elder sisters and their spouses came and Grand dad and Grand mama with Uncles Stormy, Masty and Tom – it was a full house! I got several pats on the head from them (where Horace was I didn't know nor cared!). Time came for dinner and what a spread. Mounds of food which soon disappeared,

Christmas pudding on which brandy had been poured, and I was allowed, with a lighted wick taper, to light it amid noise and cheers. Imagine if you can 22 grown ups, 5 youngsters and a baby (Millys daughter) in those two rooms getting merrier as the afternoon wore on. Dad played his concertina, sea shanties and Irish jigs! Cigar smoke and clay pipes steaming out like vapoured mists. We children let off the hook to caper as we wished. All Christmas night and well into Boxing Day the party went on, singing, dancing eating and drinking as we youngsters fell exhausted into sleep and were packed off upstairs. Such was the 1905/06 Christmas spent. I went back with Grand dad and Grand mama (bless her) and made weekly visits to Mum and Dad on Sunday nights for another year. I was due to start school in 1907 and subsequently returned home to No. 27 and Mum took me on my first day in the infants. To me, the smell of cedar and chalk still remind me of Denmark Street, even now. Kitty and Horace were my escorts to and from school and I can recall bringing home gloss paper cut outs to show how I was progressing. Miss Tarr, my teacher, was a cracker; I got on well with her. Later I was moved up into the 'big boys' class and was always in 'hot water'. I didn't want Sums or History; I wanted to be in the company of those in the Carpentry classes and aged eight. It is a very difficult age of acceptance of things, too young to be 'growed up' and too old to be a baby anymore! The sameness of life was not in keeping with my

inborn restless nature. I wanted 'adventure' and
many times, with bent intent, I found it and
sometimes it was thrust upon me. I would slope
round to Grand dads on my way home from school,
it only meant a short cut across Mills's field and I
was there. (Yes, the truth is I wanted to be
anywhere where Grand dad was!).

By now he was hitting the 65 mark, like
Grand mama. From the past he knew it as I knew it,
I should have been a good obedient boy and gone
straight home after school. The 'tanned' asses I've
had over this, but 'tis said 'Knock one devil out and
two takes his place and in those days a larruping
was a larruping, make no mistake the 'spare the rod
and spoil the child' held any water in No. 27!

It was usual that on Fridays a good attendance
ticket was given to every pupil and on producing
this to mum there was a farthing prize. No ticket –
no farthing and very often when I should have been
to school the afternoon would see yours truly down
the docks, dodging the policeman on the gate and
'Mick' would climb up gangways on to the big
ships of if the fancy took me, to the river side to see
the sailing barges. 'Red sails in the sunset' and
would long to be on one.

On one occasion, walking over the
Customhouse Bridge I came face to face with Dad,
Uncle Arthur and Stormy! Pivoting, I flew and

never stopped till I got home, a full quarter of an hour before Kitty and Horace coming home from school. Result? A questioning voice asking 'Where's the joker?' and the said 'Joker' was lashed naked to the drying rail and aching with pain, a non-stop welting and a 'Ill give you meandering around the docks Mister Joker!' until mum stopped him and a kiss 'Never mind Mick! You will not do it again, promise?'

I was to learn about keeping time and watches in an ever to be remembered episode. The Chapel was giving a 'Magic Lantern' show, a bun fight and a bag of sweets an apple and orange and we had to be at Chapel at a quarter to five. But Mick forgot this and dawdled his way home, arriving some time after 5. Kitty and Horace had already gone and I had to forfeit and go to bed early. I think that was the miserabblist (sic) night ever in my tears other than my first night in the workhouse. I really took this lesson to heart and still acknowledge that it took something like this to really teach me. I can still smell the odour of the orange breath of Horace as he came to bed and tormented me over what I had missed. But Kitty gave me some of her sweeties next day, and a farthing out of her penny. Yes, she was like this, sweet and good-natured. The times she has shielded and covered up for me are unaccountable.

I came home one day in March 1910 to find mum in tears. Dad had been taken into the seaman's hospital at the Connaught(i), located outside the Albert dock. He was in a bad way and that was the beginning of the end of our dad.

He eventually came home only to be bed ridden till he died on Saturday 26th August at 8 O'clock, just as the 'Whistle of the works' was blowing!

(i) See Note 4

Chapter Two

Life after Dad

These are moments, which forever remain a memory, Mum – brave soul, loved her George passionately, not withstanding all their fights. She washed and laid him out when the undertaker, Hitchcocks of Barking Road, came round to screw him down. We were allowed to take our last look at dad. His 'Imperial' combed and brushed and his moustache twirled defiantly still! He looked as though he was asleep. The hearse came, they carried him out of the Parlour, gently, slowly, reverently and we followed into the first coach. All the family were there and it was a 'Big send off'. I still remember the awful feeling of being frightened as he was lowered slowly into the family grave in East London Cemetery. The main mast of the family had gone. The family broke up, mom took it bravely but slowly she broke and then Grand dad 'went' – Grand mama soon followed. Kitty went into service at 2/6d a week, board and lodging, leaving Horace and I at home. Mums careful savings over the years, aided by 'subs' from the family and the selling of bits of our lovely home helped stave from the door 'The Wolf. Mum would 'char' for a few coppers 2/6d a day tid bits from the house owner till mum had to go on 'Relief'. This was the breaking point. We boys, having no one to control us took to our own ways to get by. If we wanted a meal, we simply 'nicked' it. For fuel to cook by, why, there were always big fish boxes for the taking and Id drag them home. Christmas 1911 was a cold, empty affair. We lived in the parlour and sitting room. The rest of the house was let to pay the rent – which sort of eased the situation a little. But we were in 'Poverty Street' pure and simple. Mum, liking her 'drop 'o Porter' started to drink. I will not dwell on 1911 except to say that after King Edward VII died in 1910, King George took his place and the only interesting point of this year was, when King George and Queen Mary were crowned (22 June 1911), all schools were given a mug with their portraits, a bag of sweets, some lemonade and buns, apple, orange and a days holiday. I had sort of kept up a varied attendance but when the 'wish' was on me Id be off, somewhere! Id rove the streets bare footed (you could run faster that way, and many a time after a 'snatch' I needed to). The family didn't want to know me. I would pop in to see my Uncles, a feed, perhaps a 1/2d to spend and I didn't wear my welcome out/ Christmas saw the neighbour collecting and contributing towards a dinner for us (but no invitations to joint them!) Kitty came home for Christmas Day and Boxing Day and helped to tidy the place up – I never saw her again after this.

If I went to Stratford and put my age on a bit I could get an arm badge to sell newspapers, soon you would hear me! 'STAR, all the winners, football star' (The pink 'un 1d). The weeknights were 1/2d commission, sell 3 and keep 1/2d for yourself. Fleetness of foot counted here, as competition from other 'urchins' like myself was keen. Id hit the back doubles and make 1/- to 1/3d a night which meant a lot to mum. An 'appennny bit of fish and an 'apporth of taters and an 'apporth of peas pudding and the rest for mum. I'd become a wage earner!

The capers I got up to, I'd sweep up a bucket of horse dung for 1d and there were lots of customers for this, Id knock on doors of regulars to run errands for 1/2d or 1d. The cinemas were opening in 1911; here was another avenue for cash. The manager wanted his dinner and tea brought to him. I was in for 2/6d a week and a feed thrown in! His brother drove a tram and I would collect his can of tea and bait and wait for him to come along and for this, 1/6d a week (3d a day). Playing the hop from school was down to a fine art, 2 mornings, 2 afternoons a week. Brother Horace was in Ex Seventh, the highest standard. Yours truly was at the bottom of standard Two with no hope or desire to climb the intellectual ladder. Still the loner, I chummed up with Bill Burkett, son of a seaman of dads association, occasionally I'd go to his home, be welcomed and a meal, such lovely kind people. If Bill was ever in a scrap, I'd side by him and we sort of grew 'brotherly' (He died in Merrut in India in 1925)

1911 was Prince George, our late George VI, holding his annual 'Boys camp at Southwold, and through the Fairbain Hall – a Liberal youths club – I was taken (I got Bill in as well) to a fortnight at Southwold. It was the highlight of that year. Here I could spend my days with the fishermen, help them mend their nets, splice a rope or line or tarred the keel, have a trip out to the lobster and crab pots, sleep under canvas of the camp. Join in the singsongs, it all passed too quickly for me. This hard life was hardening and shaping me, which I enjoyed. Christmas 1912 was a wee bit better than the last one for us. My sister Milly had come to stay with us and sort of kept me in line and up to Easter stayed with us. But her hubby 'Dick' came home from a long trip at sea was paid off and went to live at Harrow on the Hill.

May, June, July and August came and went, mum in her bouts of drinking was fast getting beyond keeping a grasp of things, losing her memory and, in her grief, which drink aggravated, was knocked down by a cart and taken to WhippsCross Hospital (West Ham Union) the

'Poor Law' workhouse hospital. My sister Sarah
took us boys to here home (because mum was
never to be allowed home again and was later to be
removed to Goodmayes Asylum(i) (where she died
aged 63 in 1922)). I was in Quetta India when that
happened). Horace was allowcd to lcavc school and
go to work and thereby contribute to his keep and
in this he tried to 'Boss it' over me again. The
outcome of this was a real scrap – but he was no
match for 'Mick' and it was decided to part us. Had
I known what was afoot and what was going to
happen, Id have been away – ta ta....

Sarah spruced me up and in Horaces togs,
took me to Leytonstone and into this strange place,
handed me over, kissed me and simply flew out of
the door! Two big men came into the little room
(or rather, cell) I was in, grabbed an arm each and
marched me down corridors of cold green tiled
bricks.'Slam' went the heavy iron barred door and
my clothes were taken from me and I was given
'clobber' of coarse woven serge marked 'West
Ham Union'. I was taken to another big dormitory
like room, where other poor mites were, their heads
shaven like one sees in 'Dachau Concentration
Camp. The 'Pig eared' barber came in and close

(i) See Note 5

dropped me then. I asked him 'Where am I please?' and he said 'The bleedin' workhouse, that's where!'

My ego dropped to zero, I cried and kept on crying because it was my 11th birthday… (I cannot find any room in my heart for forgiveness for any of my sisters or brother Horace ever!) I will not dwell over this period, because from that moment ever more, I started to learn what life can really be like. I was glad now. I was able to be a loner, racing the streets since over 12 months past had taught me a certain amount of animal cunning, to become watchful, quick and, if I was to survive, patient. This patience was to pay big dividends where my liberty was concerned. There was no way to get out of this institution, being barred and locked in like a prison. But I learnt that if I behaved and became non resistant and could be trusted, obedient and well behaved and polite, I may get sent to 'Snaresbrook Home' in Wanstead. (It's still there believe it or not, today, being used as a hospital). I was a model of a good boy for the six probationary months in that cold hard inhospitable Workhouse and in March 1913 I was transferred to Wanstead, but that could be another Chapter of the Life as a teenager in the 2nd decade of a 'Septuagenarian'.

I have nothing to thank the Workhouse for. I did not spend one moment of happiness within its walls, only a loathing for the so called humans that made life for an unfortunate waif or urchin like me more miserable than it ever needed to be. The 'Board of Guardians' was a soulless lot, parsimonious as any Scroogian can be. Philanthropy and love of deep feeling was never one of their Christian points. Having had first hand experience of this era of this sphere of life, and if you are to believe me (or for me to believe myself) the standards had risen from Oliver Twists time, so what must it have been like then? Charles Dickens certainly drew the curtain aside on the institutions of the poor. I have much to recommend the 'Sociological Work being done by the 'Workers of the Advancement'. More strength to their elbow and please lord do so bless them for they are thine angels

Stevenage, 1977, by yours lovingly
Dad

ChapterThree

The Institution

Those two years of racing the streets, foraging for a meal or a Penny or two, were to be training which was to stand me in good stead in the future months and years ahead as you will read. Keen of eye, fleet of foot and the ability to conform to any emergency and to be able to think clearly and quickly were all the talents I had. I was to learn other 'helpers' as time evolved. When it was decided that I should be put into care, I do not know, but I was made aware of this on Monday 11th September 1911. My sister Sarah took me to the 'Union' in Leytonsowe Road and I can relive those moments of time again. We turned into the drive and before us were the arch and big black doors on which was scribed in white letters – WEST HAM UNION – (I didn't have the foggiest idea what they portended). The building looked hard, solid and forbidding even to me. A few steps up the drive and on the right of the 'big doors' was a smaller door, black with a square grill sat in it and on the portal an iron rod which said 'Pull'.

Sarah pulled the contraption and the flap opened; Sarah pushed me inside and the door clanged shut. We stood in a hall in semi-darkness. The voice spoke, Sarah put some papers in a 'hand' and the 'hand' went away. I was just able to see a long white table and a row of forms each side of the room. There were other old people sitting. There we stood waiting, in a few minutes the 'hand' returned, said a few words to Sarah whom he showed out of the door and she just went! The 'hand' gripped me and let me to another door, which opened onto a long corridor along through into a small room. Seated in a black rocking chair was a big 'Tirpitz whiskered face and piercing eyes with which he scrutinised me from toe to brow. He looked at the papers, wrote on them and then nodded to 'hand' to take me out. No words spoken and 'hand' took me through a maze of doors and corridors and we came to one on which he knocked. It opened; he pushed me in and left me. The man who had opened the door 'grabbed' (this is the correct word for it) me and put me on a form.

'Take yer boots and clothes off sonny' he said 'and 'urry up about it, I ain't got all day you know. He helped me off with my 'Togs' as he called them, which he put into a white bag to one side. 'Come on, in 'ere', and on into a small room, like a cell in which was a swivel barbers chair and sat me down, and what little hair I had was neatly sheared off with double 00 clippers. In a twinkling of and eye I was shorn of hair. 'That's better, we can see where we are now' he said and proceeded to rub some vile green ointment onto my head. 'If there's anything there, that'll be bound to shift 'em', he said with a coughing guffaw. 'C'mon sonny, into the bath', and lifting a platform by the side of the wall revealed a long bath which he started to fill by shifting a lever and in he lifted me. Even now, whenever I smell Jeyes fluid or carbolic I again remember that bath episode. The long stick cake of soap, red as a cherry and how it burnt, hot on my body and he didn't spare the lather either! He ducked me under and lifted me out onto a mat marked with the words West Ham Union in a circle. He got a big course linen towel and dried me. A knock came and he opened the door to receive a pair of rope-soled shoes (like the Chinese wear), a pair of shorts and a red flannel vest. 'Put these on sonny. I was on the verge of shock tears by now.

'Where am I?' I asked

'Where are you? Why, in the bleeding Workhouse of course, where else?'
I started to cry then and was to cry for a long time after, until there were no more tears.

I had heard Grand dad and Daddy with my Uncle speak of the Workhouse and my dear Mum saying what a dreadful place it must be (Please god I never go there). It is a good job we know not of our destiny. Poor Mum, but at least you had food and clean sheets in Goodmayes, and no worries of the hard outside world. You see loves, why I hate my brother and sisters and others of the family too. Yet mum, you were better off in the end xxx. We both, in our different ways, got by! Yet a club round each week and our Milly to look after you, there were enough of the family to do this but were you too far gone to help? I've often wondered this over in my mind and still am without a tangible answer except to say 'It was meant to be' Peace be with you Mummy love.

I thought of you that day, I cried for you, not understanding what it was all about. The voice said roughly 'It's no use crying boy, that won't help' and he pulled a rope and a knock came at the door. He opened the door, beckoned me and handed me over to someone else. Along more corridors and through doors until we came to a pair of glass doors which led to a long big room which contained other boys, some younger, some a little older than I. A woman in a dark blue uniform with a white starched apron the white banded hat of a nurse met us and took the slip of paper and pushes me in after unlocking the door. I was in. The other little chaps came up to this new arrival and stared, stared and stared. 'Wots 'e crying for, wotcha crying for, lost yer mum? Eh?' and I sloshed him and stood ready to do battle! A big boy 'Heideborg' by name as it turned out (he was No. 1 headman) pushed his way to me, made a pass and I hit him. Low and hard and as he doubled up I swiped him again, two-handed chop on his thick neck and down he went, first on his knees and then on his face! There was a stampede! 'Nurse, nurse' rose the cry. Nurse James (who was later to come to Snaresbrook) came in and as the 'yobs' point turns to me and makes a pass grab at me. I wasn't there though was I? As she stumbled forward I backed away. One kiddo came up behind me and folded his arms around me saying 'I got 'im, I got 'im'. Like hell he had! I held his hands in mine, bent forward, took a step forward and straightened up and turned letting go of his hands and cuffed him solid. Away to the left he sailed and on the semi polished bee wax floor, slid, zoom! The nurse pounced again and missed. My paddy was up by now, Heideborg got up and I made a bee line for him head on and the two of us went down, whump! My sandal slippers had left my feet and I had a fair bearing on my feet, but was piled on and held, but some short punches caused some 'Ouches'! I was made secure and hatched down; face down, with my legs sat on, one on my head. I was clued fore and aft proper. I was held like that hardly getting air into my lungs and lay ever so still. I suddenly, for the want of air, 'humped' my arse and up and away sailed the chappie on my back. But I was not to get loose. My hands were sought and tied behind my back and, like Samson, pulled up to my feet and literally carried to the form which ran all the way around the big room. I was sat down, more nurses appeared and a conflab started between them. A uniformed man came in and came over, stood me on my feet and asked me 'What started you off boy?' and I told him of what the yobs had said about my Mum and me. He looked at the boy and shook his head, 'Shouldn't have done that boy' he said, and 'you'll get into trouble one of these days if you don't watch out!' He grinned and said as an aside 'As if he hasn't already haw haw haw' 'Say you are sorry to him' and he waved to 'Kiddo' to do the same. I saw the easy way out and said sorry and 'Kiddo said sorry too. He then instructed us to shake hands, he untied me and we shook hands as if nothing had happened. Nurse James shooed them of with 'Now go and play children'. She took me into the office with Mr. Uniform. I was told to sit down and was asked my name and my age. I said 'I'm ten on Wednesday'. She looked at 'Uniform' with a shake of her head 'Tch tch, had I any brothers and sisters?' I told her and this back and forth chitchat set me to crying again 'I want to go home' 'There there' she replied 'don't cry, you will go home again soon. Come now, promise me there will be no more fighting and be a good boy, yes?' I said 'Yes ma'am' (nods and shakes of heads were never allowed by Dad – 'You've a tongue in your head son!') Uniform and Nurse James took me back into the big room but none came near me now, Nr. 1 was glowering at me but look for look, he'd turn his head first! I went and sat on the side forms, 'Monkey', as he was to become afterwards, brought my sandals and sat beside me, a grin on his 'Monkey face'. (I learned to love him!)

'Wotcher name? He asked in his diatribe cockney. I said 'Micky Jennings'

'Where you from?' 'Canning town, my aunt lives there'

'What part?' From then on we were inseparable, we talked, sat, played, ate at meal times, slept next to each other and in a scrap he was a terrier, fast and nimble, he could run like a hare! But more of him later. We sat and chatted until the dinner bell sounded and we filed into the dining room. One long table, 12 either side. No. 1 at the top end, he conducted grace, when to begin, when to get up and he got extra tid bits for doing this. The 'kiddos' were scared of him, even 'Monkey' (Bill Berkett his name I learnt), and when he said 'You ain't scared of him Mick are you?' I laughed and said 'No, I'm not and I don't want you to be either and I was to caution No. 1 to lay off or else.

Dinner was Shepherds Pie and Bread Pudding, good and tasty but not enough, I was always hungry, we all were really! Grace said, we filed out into the big room, no organised games, just boredom. The afternoon, with early darkening nights coming on, the big bare room with its white washed walls and green painted half way up chill, uninviting and miserable, which in turn made me miserable too. I missed the freedom of racing the streets and all that it meant. We were forgotten children, no toys, and no sweets. Let me out of here, I was very easy on 'turning the tap on, crying. I was sobbing internally. When tea time came and we had coarse workhouse bread and dripping, one and a half slices of doorstep, 6'' x 4' lobbed at us and a mug of cocoa, thick, unsweetened which of course we became used to and which soon disappeared into gobs ever hungry. We were given a quarter of an hour to have tea then we filed out to wash in the big trough, cold water and the accursed carbolic soap. Inspection at 4.45, up to bed in the big 25 a side dormitory with its gas lit lamp in the centre and at each end of the room, behind a glass panel (I was to see the same kind in 'nick' in later years). This was a 'night light' precaution against fire and which acted as a look in spy for the night rounds vigilante. We folded out 'togs' at the foot of the bed on the floor, put on a long night gown of stiff cold linen, knelt by our iron bed and prayers were said by No. 1,'Our Father etc and bless us this night 'till morning light appears Amen'. We'd jump into bed, no talking. If anyone was caught talking they were made to stand on the cold floor in the middle of the room and on the second offence, naked. No, to talking. All this, so strange to me in the cold sheets in the quiet I lay and then Id cry every night was the same until there were no more tears to shed.

Wednesday came it was my birthday, how miserable I was, I think now it was my most ever miserable day. If someone had poked fun at me because I was sad, I would have killed them! Then started the restlessness of getting out and free again. I was to mention this to 'Monkey' who told me of the chance of getting to Snaresbrook(i), the other home for kids like us. Only the 'right' type of good behavioured (sic) boys were sent there. The other places weren't much cop. Believe me in this, it was the only time in my life except for 'Stirling' that I was on my best behaviour.My brother Horace came to see me on a Sunday in October and again in November and told me that Sarah had said she would have me home for Christmas. This cheered me up and I looked forward to it, but Christmas came and went and I didn't go home. I've never 'lived' that out of my mind inside me still burns a hate Ill never lose. The only satisfaction I have is that her husband George Brooks was mortally wounded by a bomb and took a long time to die. Sarah was to know what loneliness is without a friend in the world. To it came home to her. But that Christmas was a cold 'Charity' one, an apple, an orange and a few pear drops, but they were accepted, better than nothing!

March came and with it a good report:
'Tractable, willing, bright, a well behaved boy'

(i) See Note 6

Monkey and I along with or. 1 and four others were on our way to Snaresbrook Hall!

We were taken there in the Brake van, something like a Black Maria, and I shall never forget as we lined up to go, all excited to leave. As we went through the big black gates, down the short drive where six months ago I had trotted up beside Sarah. To hear other voices, hear different noises. The clang of the trams, the clip clop of the horses, it is not so far away. Past the Green Man, across the wide flats through Woodford and on to the north side of Wanstead. About an hours ride yet it was the sweetest ride of my life, then and since! The Brake pulled up and the large trellis wrought iron gates of the hall swung open, we had arrived!

Chapter Four

Changing times

I must take a 'break' here, to retrack back, to put a clearer picture to the reader.

It would take long hours of reading and study, volumes of details of affairs which led to the veil being drawn aside by Charles Dickens and his characters and conditions then prevailing in his 'Oliver Twist'. The reader would be informed by reading the 'ARTCLES OF POOR LAW REFORM of 1834 sic 1723/68 which instituted that each borough be responsible for its own poor by means of 'Parish Relief', the forerunner of the means test. The mortality rate and paupers burials being a great burden on the parishes. Circa Disraeli, Peel and Russell, the first reform bill 181 caused many a raised eyebrow and tut tutting among the autocracy. But the radical change had come to stay and the chartists were going to keep it that way, because since Pitt and the mutiny of Spithead and hope they had worked long and hard to better conditions for the working population. No more would the few hold reins over the poor. The onus of looking after the poor had been destriously moved to borough councils who set up a board of guardians to control, issue and relieve any 'Destitued Person or Child' etc. etc.

It was left to those 'Responsible' people to use, as they thought necessary, such help, assistance as was deemed appropriate. The said 'Guardians' were to say the least of "puritanical and parsimonious habits, but a chartist here and there kept them moving along the lines of reform, reform and still more reform. There were five hospitals in all London to cover the needs of the people, Guys, St. Barts, St Thomas', St. George and East London. Later each borough built their own voluntary aided hospitals, one of the first being the Elizabeth Garrett in Euston (she was incidentally the first woman to hold an MD (France 1901).

Splinter groups of voluntary aid (Nurse Nightingale emulating 'Nell Gwynne's' Chelsea Hospital (RH) set about society to help the children, so came into being Dr. Barnados Homes, Shaftsbury Homes, Waifs and Strays – Ragged School Union (which still exists today) London growing richer every day from Empire trading and expanding in population too. There were bound to be drop outs, misfortune and poverty. Rich 'humanitarian' boroughs were busy in the background, building institutions go house and shelter the homeless, aged and infirm and 'lunatics caused by drink. There was a pub or gin place of off license every 100 yards or so). Charringtons, Courage, Whitbread and combination brewers, Watneys, Combe and Reid etc. etc., they all had a good trade opening at 5am until midnight. Thus William Booths Salvation Army 'anti beer trade' came into being, with their halfpenny 'War Cry' editions. Drink was to cause more poverty than could be contained into these institutions.

Into the Poor Law Institutions, Infirmaries and Asylums came the poor, it was either there or prison so there was really no choice about it. The streets were roamed by urchins, 'Mites-Brats' were pretty prevalent then and there was very little help or pity shown. SoWest Ham Union came to be built in 1850-1880 (and it is still in existence, being only known now as a hospital (A rose by any other name)). This edifice, built in 160 acres of land, spewed out left, right and centre and could house a thousand easily. Completely self contained, having its own bakery, laundry and other activities for its maintenance for East and West Ham (the Hamlets as is now known), were rich with a higher rate value than many neighbouring boroughs. Be that as it may, its board of guardians were of the run of the mill type, prevailing then. Pinch penny parsimonious and very suspicious, believing that they only catered for thieves. Everything was built to last, the initial cost of it was to last donkeys years (mind you, there were some light fingered 'no principles' about so we mustn't criticise too much). Austerity was one of the main points. Everything that could be scrubbed white was white, with the ever prevailing John Knights (soap makers) carbolic. Everything was substantial and heavy. Linen was Irish and 1st quality, made to stand a hiding. Food was of good quality and none was wasted, any left overs either hashed and served up again or given to the pigs. Yes, there was even their own piggery too. There were cows for milking, kept on a holding in a nearby field (Mills field). The Infirmary was a long block at the back of the building, the men's block and the women's block, girls block and boys block. A quadrangle and reception, it looked for all the world like a prison, bars and all! There were two mortuaries, one on the female side and one on the male, even in death the sexes were kept apart.

Once inside and the reception door clanged shut it would be fair to say there was perhaps only one thing missing, I imagine the words, written in black on a green background with a white surround 'Give up hope all who enter these portals'. For such would be a fair summary of the Workhouse. From the mists of recollection of a young mind entails no effort on my part, they are too imprinted to forget. After two years of racing the streets of freedom the incarceration the big room and its dormitory, the dry cold smell of carbolic is still with me. The sameness of the days and nights, the meals, the sitting on those white scrubbed side forms. There was no schooling, no teaching, except the rule 'Obedience, Submissiveness and Quietness'. Sundays, with its reading of the bible by the nurse on duty, monotonous and boring, the Tea was the only highlight to look forward to. In place of bread and dripping we were give two slices of 'Seedy' bread (Caraway seeds) made like a cake. A rare treat and sometimes a spot of jam too! I used to nibble this to make it last a long time, enjoying every crumb, wetting my fingers to pick up any crumbs which had fallen on the scrubbed table – scrumptious. Sometimes there would be an apple to slowly munch, seeds, stalk and all and any of the other boys discarded apple cores too. I liked Tuesdays too, it was thick brown stew day! Bits of fatty meat in it, wholesome and tasty, but to a growing lad the 'Oliver Twist' touch was ever present at every meal.

Breakfast was always number one for me, a bowl of oatmeal with its strong bitter taste and oh so thick. I was always full, supping up the 'don't waste it' and leftovers of the other boys. There was no sugar, only flavoured by salt and it went down a treat. Now and again there would be 'Fowlers' black treacle on your bread. Any and everything edible was joyfully received and disposed of; as mum was wont to say 'Gratefully received and thankfully accepted'. Those six months taught me patience and to curb the 'Paddy' in me that was always near the surface due to my pent up emotions and the frustrated feeling of being caged. I was to start another phase in Snaresbrook Hall. In procedures there wasn't much difference, the routine was to be the same except we were allowed, weather permitting, to walk around the grounds outside. Semi-free to talk openly, to see the girls and shyly glance at them, but never to co-ed except when on open visiting days. On those days they came into our block to visit their brothers or brothers to visit their sisters on a Sunday. Strict decorum ruled the standing order. So, this leads me back to my narrative of entering through those high trellis ornamental gates in the brake van.

Chapter Five

Snaresbrook Hall

The driver 'Giddy upped' the horses in a slow walk along the long drive past A and B blocks (girls section), past the resident Superintendents house to C block. Nurse James, who had accompanied us, got down from the brake when the exit door was opened and three of us boys, Monkey, Heideborg and myself alighted (the other three went do D block). The driver, leaning over from his seat, waved at us and we waved back. Nurse James, along with another nurse, shepherded us up some steps into the hall, with its black and white square tiled floor. We went into another high long day room and were made to sit (believe it or not) on side forms, which went all the way around the room, on which sat the other 'residents. They, like us, were close cropped. After a short while we were taken for a bath (why, I will never know, we'd had one before we left the Union). Our cloths were changed and we were given others, the ones we had taken off were collected and put in white bags, presumably to be returned to Leytonstone.

After ablutions we were sent back to the day room. This was a much brighter and sunnier room, with long windows (unbarred!) and you could look out onto the lawns. What a vast difference in feeling it gave. The other boys were brought to us and introduced to us by name, a friendly atmosphere was present.

'Monkey' was enjoying himself and as for me, I did not feel so 'keyed up', losing a lot of the animal suspicion I had had in Leytonstone. I felt relaxed, occasionally looking out of the window that beckoned me to freedom. I looked to the far boundary, weighing up certain ground and cover points. I was not to know it but I too was being watched by keen covert eyes as to my reactions. This I was to find out when I heard the words 'Not thinking of running away boy are you? We have big dogs out there!' Perhaps in the past others had tried and lost but I put on my most subservient voice and replied 'No sir! I was only looking; it's so different from the other place isn't it?' This explanation seemed to satisfy the voice (or did it?)

Dinner was called by a bell, we trooped in, grace was said and we ate a tasty 'Dry hash' corned beef and potatoes, followed by jam duff. We were left to our own devices in the afternoon to await tea, which was bread and syrup, but still the same 1 and a half slices and cocoa. 5 o'clock came and it was 'wash and bed', the routine was the same as

Leytonstone, prayers, a long gown and we could chat until 5.30 then lights out and settle down. Deep inside me I was excited, inches away from me was freedom, via the big window. A drop of 18 to 20 feet and I'd be gone. It was a pipe dream after all, the window was too heavy to lift, the bushes beneath were Gorse and Laurel. If only I could have opened the window – ah well! I eventually got over my disappointment. I was to wait until the next week and we were taken to J block, a building at the end of block D which was a schoolroom. Here was a toilet, which had a door leading from it, but the snag was, when you wanted to 'Please sir, may I go?' a 'big boy' was sent with you and there was little chance of ever getting past him. I told 'Monkey' of this and he came up with the idea of becoming a monitor, of helping the nurses with little jobs. As I have stated before I was classed as a 'willing boy' and Monkey and I became two of the most willing, well behaved boys Snaresbrook ever had! For two months we played this game and vigilance over us slowly relaxed. We were allowed, at first, to go out the back to help clean boots (a skein of oil blackening, you had to spit on and rub into the boots and then polish them). Lots of other little helps cropped up, little tid-bits to be had and we became trusted, to be allowed out on walk abouts in the front area. I even developed a slow slouchy walk and being told of this many times, 'Walk smartly!' During gym exercise I would appear sloppy, heavy, unbalanced and awkward.

Our scheme was to deceive sharp ever watching eyes. 'Piggy' Gilbert, he of the large ears, was our instructor in the gym; I could never jump the horse, couldn't climb the bars, and always had a heavy laboured run, lagging behind the others. Monkey played his part to perfection, we were known as the sluggards, useless and therefore hardly worth watching and so things relaxed.

When we were ready we decided to ask to 'Please sir, may I?' and the answer was 'Yes, but don't be long!' Out we walked, through the lavatory door and whoom! Over a fence and away, away like the hammers of hell, far away by nightfall in Woodford. We hid in a barn until morning and knowing my bearings, jumped on a 'country wagon' going to Barking and lay doggo. At about 12 o'clock we were nigh there and we got off and got our bearings, we were near Dagenham then, in the country, all fields as it was then. We made our way to Dagenham docks, and scrounged round the

barges. We found a chap who gave us some bread and tea but our haircuts made him suspicious 'Where are you kids from, borstal?' he asked. Monkey replied 'Nah, we bunked out of the workhouse' (Tell the bloke the truth and he wont believe you!), he didn't and asked us where we lived. Monkey told him that we didn't have a home and no one to help us. The chap let us sleep on the barge that night and gave us some breakfast the following morning along with tuppence each. He told us we might get a job helping out with potato picking at his brothers farm up the road and he took us there. We slept in a barn in the straw and helped with the 'tater picking' for a fortnight. We got seven shillings and sixpence each and left to make our way to Tilbury. We were two days getting there and we crossed over on the ferry to Gravesend, from there we made our way to Faversham and the hop gardens owned by Whitbreds. There were many families from South London, living in huts, picking hops. We fitted ourselves in to hide here for the season.

We enjoyed the rough and ready conditions, no questions asked. We were just two poor kids, like many around us. Homeless 'poor little sods'. These hop pickers were a kindly generous people and gave unselfishly to others who were not so well done by. When the season ended we had cash and got a lift back on the train to London Bridge and a fourpenny ride on a number 40 bus took us right home to Canning Town. We were on home ground here. A penny a night 'kip house', coffee shops to eat in and we were free! At least we thought we were until the 'Bobbies' walked into the 'kip house' on a seek and search mission for some one and we were trapped! As easy as that! We were taken to Lansdown police station where we owned up to being out of the workhouse (they knew who we were already by our descriptions). We were

63

kept in a cell until two chaps came from
Snaresbrook to collect us; we were put in a van and
taken back. I gave the money I had to the chap as it
was no use to me any more. Getting back we were
close cropped again, scrubbed, and I don't mean
maybe (have you ever been scrubbed with a hemp
brush? Well don't! I can't recommend it). We had
missed tea but were given the usual, and that cocoa
was the nicest warmish drink I've ever had. This
time we were to be kept in a solitary cell, I
remember crying again all night. The next day we
went, in disgrace, before the superintendent, a very
imposing military person. He sentenced us both to
be birched and duly birched we were and a week in
the cells. This only made me more determined to
get out again and stay out.

Monkey was sent to the training ship
Cornwall(i) at
Purfleet and I was told that if I didn't behave in the
future I'd be sent there too. It was music to my
ears; they couldn't have threatened me better! I
became a real 'sod' in the true sense of the word
and was eventually despatched after two weeks to
the Cornwall. It was close though, it was a toss up
between the Cornwall and the Mount
Edgecombe(ii) in Edgecombe Bay in Devon. My
reception on the long boat which had been sent to

(i)   See Note 7
(ii)   See Note 8

bring me aboard was a clout with a 'Short end' and the words 'Sit here boy and sit still'. On board the Chief Petty Officer stood on the quarter deck and told them to take me below. I was booted down the companion way between decks and thrown into the small cell. I shall leave the reader here because my next letter is again a lengthy one and because I do not wish my narrative to become boring. Suffice to say that those suspended hours of life wasted in what was meant to be 'Humane and Beneficial' to a waif and stray, a mite, a brat, like me, was wasted really. I could still think or would like to, have got by yet out of decency I must thank them for their good and goodly intentions and for taking care of me. They were not to know of my heart and mind and where they lay, only that they engraved in and on them something I can never forget, ever!
They set me on a road, destined for me, a small faction in life's training and this I shall not regret, for every little helps.

Should the reader wish to know of the next chapter I can comply, setting down only facts and not conjecture.
Today's modern method of correction is so different from my 'time' and it is left to the future to see its results. It is a different world to the one in

which I lived, where to just 'get by' was enough. The old 'Reformers' would indeed be pleased to see the social amenities as they are today. This was their aim, to abolish Pawn shops, Pubs and Penury, they have nearly arrived. It is the corrective 'Do gooders' which should have another re-think. A little training and coercion for the drug taker (for the drug pusher, a quick and sudden death), on a 'Training ship' short and sharp lesson and plenty of 'Aloft' and rowing and clean exercise would stop all desire of the transcendental lark! For the juvenile delinquent, a touch of 'Stirling' wouldn't be amiss either with 'Plenty more of where that came from' and of hard tack and hard boards to lie upon and hard heavy hours and 'Hard Luck' chum!

Chapter Six

T.S. CORNWALL

8th February 1975

In Gravesend, close by the old pier, stands a Georgian house of great beauty. It was once a waiting and rest house for captains and admirals of H.M. Navy (circa 1758) onwards who were coming ashore or waiting to go to sea. This later became the pilot's house, housing both river and deep sea pilots, awaiting ships to the docks upriver or down the pipeline, the channel. Today it is used as a training school for entrants into the merchant service or navy and took over the duties of the one time training ships such as HMS Warspite, Arithiusa and Cornwall which lay in Erith Reach abaft Gravesend. In Nelsons day Purfleet was a naval 'rest up' above Tilbury fortress, my old Depot ship of the Great War. HMS Eagle lay there as a prison ship for the Dutch enemy. It was used as a 'Press station' ashore during he times of the press gangs between 1650 and 1818. There has always been a ship there of some kind, and in my time the Warspite, a Shaftesbury Homes Ship, the Arethusa, a Royal Navy establishment ship and the truant ship of correction Training Ship Cornwall. They were all full rigged ships of the line of some 69 guns, big chappies, who had been pensioned off to train sailors, civil or naval. They were manned by pensioned navel men of the old school, hard, rough and tough chaps of 25 years service who knew every inch of the vessels, all sails from Fore Jib to Mizzen, of Top Royals, Fore Royals all Royals, Top Gallants, Fore and Aft Main to the big Main sheets. There was nothing they did not know. It was nice as a visitor on Trafalgar day to see the ships dressed overall with bunting, gaily coloured up. Yet, the visitor was not aware of the training undergone before this was possible. The visitor would not be aware of the sod searing agony of the crew (although we had it easy in comparison to Nelsons time, which must have been sheer hell for them). They looked what they were, stately, majestic, forbidding and solid. All black with white gun ports. Real guns too, solid heavy blighters, yet they were babies in comparison to H.M Victory, a 120 gunner whose anchor line was twelve inches thick (splice that bastard!), yet 'twas done.

It was to the Cornwall I was rowed out to, by sturdy clean looking eager youngsters of 11, 12, 13 or 14 years of age, all dressed in round rig, chin straps secured by blue tape against the wind and tide. WEN-TWO-THREE 'feather', a press on the

68

grip, back to WEN-TWO-THREE, their little young bodies, eyes fixed on the neck of the rower in front, bodies leant back as the bladed oar clipped three inches in to the water. WEN-TWO, a long steady pull, a twist of the wrist –THREE- down three inches n the hands, a half turn upwards to feather the blade, a lean forward, pushing the blade to arms length away from you and a twist inwards of the wrist. WEN, dip, TWO, pull, till the shaft touched the chest, a twist of the wrist, THREE… You could have timed a clock by the steady rhythm, the shaft in the rowlocks 'weee-d-shup-wee'd as the leather hide met the steel of the rowlocks edge. The coxswain at the tiller, eyes about him, tugged the line on steerage facing the boats crew. The Bosun in the prow, eyes about WEN-TWOing.

'Number for, put your back into it! Number six, lay a little!' It was Wilson the bosun who had encouraged me on board with a ropes end in my ribs. I sat amid ships like some prisoner, facing aft and becoming a little chilled by the wind off the river. The long boat pulled way ahead and was allowed to drift backwards on the tide which was on the ebb. We drifted past and starboard, sculls upright with the port culls, pulling, laid along side the 'gaff way', a kind of stairway running up the side of the ship. To me, she seemed enormous. We made fast and I was the first aboard, followed by the bosun. At the top stood the Master-at Arms, a real bruiser, he just said 'Take him below' and the bosun shoved me toward the companion way, giving me a 'sender' of a kick. Headlong I travelled and saved myself from falling, grabbing the hand line. I slithered down those brass studded steps until I touched bottom deck, Bosun right behind me. He pushed me into a wee 'cell' pulled the door shut and hooked a chain on the side and went away. If you had put a cat in there with me it would have been crowded. I could smell tar, suffocatingly so, but it was warm, yes, warmer than that Long John of a boat. I sat on a hatchway which was suspended by two ropes, it was dark down there, but after a while my eyes got accustomed o the semi- gloom. I could hear the water lapping against the bulkhead. From outside a voice said 'Get that rig off you' it was so sudden I jumped. 'Come on, look lively' I knew what rig was (thank you Grand dad) so I undressed and waited... and waited... and waited. Not a sound except the lapping water. I waited for what seemed ages though it was but minutes. The chain jiggled, the door opened. 'Out here, lively now' and I stepped out. 'Pick these up and get back lad' (we were always 'Lads'), and I collected a bundle of togs, which turned out afterwards to be a full kit. Jumper, Collar, Flannel vest, Lanyard, Bell bottomed trews. 'Get back in and get dressed' which I did pretty pronto I can tell you. Somehow I felt happy, happier than I'd been for many a long day. I was on a real ship, a 'Man 'o War'. My childhood dreams had come true. 'Grand dad, I'm here!' Could any child be happier? They can do what they like to me, I don't care now (and I kept that attitude for twelve solid months 'till I scarpered' on my third trip ashore). I often wondered if I'd done the right thing then, but we re not masters of our destiny, it was to be, yes?

This cell lark was to accustom you, like quieten you down, and subdue you, the first part of brain washing for the future. I was subdued alright, I was happy – who cares! Bosun brought some stew in a basin and a chunk of delicious ships baked bread and I say a chunk, I mean a chunk! One of Grand dads chunks, which would fill a horse up. No spoon, piping hot, I blew on it and dunked my bread in it, boy was I ready for it. A little later a voice said
'Want some more lad?'
'Yes please sir'
I was ladled out another basin full.
'Excuse me sir, where do I pee?'
'Down the sump in the corner'
Which I found to be a scupper hole which drain off seas shipped off down the companion way. Okay, my no. 2's went down there too along with any water when the 'Devils cabin' is hosed out. I heard a ships bell, -CLANG-DONG- CLANG- 3 bells which I judged to be 1.30. I was to hear that bell every waking hour. Our work hours were governed by it, all our 'Stations' were by it, which I learnt off by heart. We were told once and once only, made to repeat orders so we

understood what was expected of us (You know that one, England expects every man this day to do his duty – right then let's see it is done then!) Now then my lovely Grand dad, your teaching hadn't fallen on a stupid mind and deaf ears. I was to be called a 'Bright Lad' on the way I clued onto instruction (little did they know I'd had years of 'Ships drill' and I never did let on that I had had keel training from a real Tar! Did I Grand dad). You must have had many a chuckle at 'Mick' being made (and I don't mean maybe) into a son of a sailor. All you taught me was going to pay a handsome dividend.

'Finished Lad? Then let's have the basin back'

And I handed it over with a

'Thank you sir'

'Don't call me sir, call me Bosun, you say sir to the Master-at-Arms or ships Officers, got it lad?'

'Yes Bosun' And he laughed

'Sure, got it off pat haven't you?'

And he clanged the chain on the door. I heard 4 bells, 5, 6, 7 and at 8 bells I heard a scampering of noise, away aft of me. It was the ship's crew coming down below. The chain clanked again Wilson (Tug) put in some chunks of bread and a dob of ships marmalade and a basin of thick cocoa (we never did have tea at any time, always cocoa, navy style. You have to drink ships navy cocoa to know what I am writing about, there is certain solidness and taste about it which you never ever lose. The memory of its smell, quite unique in itself. It is filling warming and satisfying. Ships jam and marmalade, out of tins is the same. Margarine has a salty taste too… Ships grub was proper grub, to eat and enjoy to your fullness. On Fridays you had ships biscuits four inches square and one inch thick, hard tack, with salt beef or Newfoundland cod. I still recall the 'Menu'; good plain wholesome grub and plenty of it too. Tasty 'Hashes' of Corned Beef and spuds and onions. Jam Duff, Treacle Duff, marmalade Duff. Roly Poly, baked and done to a turn. After the workhouse it was a lords feast I can assure you. The Dumpling stews with curried fat pieces of meat, talk about 'Blow yer kit out' yet we carried no surplus fat on our lean ribs. The healthy clambering up aloft, the holy stoning, rowing and P.T to keep us on our toes and fit! You have never done 'Quarter Staves' have you? Never pulled a Long John boat, scrambled aloft, cat walked the spars, unfurled the sheets (sails). Clue 'em up, unclue and re-furl them. You have never been on your hands and knees, holy stoning the decks, or picked oakum as a '10a' punishment, 2 pounds of it until the skin comes off of your finger tips, or shivered out on a spar, way up in the 'angels Tops' and all of this done by the Boson's whistle (a little curled silver thing hung around his neck on a silver chain, which takes an apt man to Pipe each note, each of which meant such and such). You have never been 'gee'd up' with a ropes end. And so, you have never lived! Have you ever been cut down in your hammock, you head hope severed by a deft stroke of a cutlass, to go tumbling out on the deck six feet below (and then have to splice it again) just because you didn't get out

lively on the first shake, to 'show a leg there' (an heritage of Nelsons days). Have you ever seen some poor sod run the gauntlet? The tunnel of ropes ends? Or witnessed someone spread eagled on a St. Georges cross and shipped, both definitely a sure cure all for dad feelings and disobedience I can assure you! I had heard stories of the old days from Grand dad with Grand mama nodding and smiling at the narratives with the aside;

'You may run into these yourself Mick, and see for yourself one day' Well, the 'one day' had arrived, I was in 'chokey' to prove the factum of the point. I was, in the future, to recall what my tutor had said, but even then we had it sort of tempered cushy compared to the olden days. Being youngsters counted for a lot I suppose but the hard strict laws were maintained and administered. Do that which you shouldn't do and you would suffer the consequences accordingly! I was given a white navy blanket to cover me and was told to pipe down for the night in the pitch dark on the hard hatch cover which was to be my bed for three nights. On the fourth day aboard the voice said;

'Lad, spruce yourself up, you are for muster to ships office,'

This was to be before no. 1, The first lieutenant before I went into the captains office. Coming as I did from the semi-gloom up the companion way into broad daylight so sudden like caused me to shut my eyes and falter in my step. A clouter with the 'starter' always at hand with the boson as the worthy wielder started me again! I was marched 'tween the assembled crew to and past the Quarter deck, that holy of holies, past the mainmast to the Master-at-Arms, standing awaiting 'defaulters muster'.

'Halt, right turn, cap off stand still'

I stood still, you bet. There were three defaulters that bright sunny morning. The ships bell clanged out two strokes, it was 9 o'clock (it was always known as 'Doom hour'). The three defaulters were dispensed with and then it was my turn. 'Left turn, right wheel, quick march'

And in I trooped.

'Halt, right turn, Rating Jennings sir!'

The captain, dressed all over in nr. Ones, gold braided and keen of eye, he looked at me and then the sheaf of papers on his desk.

'Ah yes, so, you ran away from the institution did you. Well, you won't run away from here will you?'

Prompted by a poke in the back from the Master-at-Arms I replied

'No Sir, I want to be a sailor sir'

'Oh you do, do you? Lets see his wishes are carried out Master-at-arms, take him out'.

It was over in seconds, getting outside again I was taken and put into line with the other members awaiting inspection muster. On the stroke of 3 bells the Captain and his First Lieutenant and Master-at-Arms along with the Boson walked down and keenly inspected each one of us in turn. When he came to me he smiled enough to say 'well, you have started well, stay that way'. All saluted him and boson piped morning stations. There was a scattering of the crew, groups going to the various points of morning stations. I was lost, standing alone, real lost! All about me was bustle and I stood still, not even daring to turn my head. Stock still and that took determination. Wilson came up and said 'See where you are standing, mark it well, because that is your station muster spot from now on. So, come along now, we do everything at a lively trot her lad' And he broke into a trot, easy like and I was take to the ships doctor. I was examined, asked to tell him what colours I could see on a round disc, that was the shape, what was that and so on. I was passed fit for ships duties! Wilson took me below decks and showed me my Mess, No. 16. I was shown where I was to sit at meals and he gave me a lecture of behaviour at meals and the warning;

'You are never to go to any other Mess!'

The 'table' was two feet wide and ten feet long, hooked up by pulley lines flush to the bulkhead and forms treated the same way, being fastened to the bulkhead by swivel clips. I was shown my hooks on which I had to sling my hammock on and went to ships stores to draw a 'Ditty Box', a blanket, a hammock, a 'Housewife' of needles and thread, two blocks of wood with my name on, one in black the other in white (used to label my 'togs). I also received a No. 1 'Duck suit' (white), a pair of shoes (by the way, I was bare footed, all work being done in bare feet), a pair of blue woollen socks and a jersey. I carried all these at a lively trot ('twas ever thus) back to my niche in the Mess and was shown how to stow them. This done, I was taken on deck again and shown where no. 16 mess lads were engaged on 'holy stoning' a section of the top deck or 'Poop' and introduced to my ship (Mess) mates and was put straight to work until cocoa break at 6 bells. The start and end of the 10 minute break being signalled by the pipe. At the end of the break it was back at a lively trot to finish our once a week job on the 'Poop'. Every Mess to turn and turn about, a roster (ah, that name, roster). There was a roster for everything and for this particular job we had a bar of black ships chocolate after Prayer Muster on Sunday. A real treat I can assure you (seeing as it was only four times a year except for Trafalgar day which was gala sports and bun fight day). I took part in two actually, No. 16 Mess tie with No. 8 Mess for 2nd place. No's 1 and 2 (The seniors Mess, who were never beaten) were the winners of the trophy, a replica of the Victory (rather apt don't you think?). The hard and fast rule, not talking or inattention during lecture lessons and working allowed, but we got used to that and a lot more besides. Galley was piped at 2 bells (one o'clock) for a 30 minute break and piped to afternoon stations which was a per roster and very varied, but also very easy until 8 bells (four o'clock – everything being Greenwich time). We had one hours school (seamanship) one hour deck seamanship half and hour of afloat seamanship. The time soon passed, sometimes too quickly for me at any rate. I loved every minute aboard the Cornwall. I rose to be no. 2 stroke in the Long John and normally this was a three or four year accomplishment. I was a demonstrator at rope classes, helping the instructor in knots, splices, warping and tucking. Standing in front of the class demonstrating what the instructor said. I could 'bunting' the code flags, any job on board. I had a pass in all tests except arithmetic and Logarithms. I could 'box' the compass, lay a course lay off the sheets, yes, I was home! I was in my element, but like the heartburn I'd have a yearning for 27 Croydon Road or 287 Hermit Road. Sometimes I became really homesick when I lay in my hammock 'till sleep came. There was no way ashore, no way out and I accepted it as such. The winter days shortened, the nights 'tween decks longer but ships routine never varied. 'Show a leg' was piped at 4 bells (6 am), a strip off sluice followed, lash up and sow hammocks, a basin of cocoa and at 5 bells it was time to shine and show, cleaning the Mess and table and forms, getting things ship shame and Bristol fashion. Mess inspection by the Master-at-Arms and Boson followed at 7 bells, then it was on deck for P.T. summer or winter! Sluggards were twiced (sic) over the crows nest, last man down over again. There were no favourites aboard, it was all on merit alone. No 'blue eyes' or 'pansies', no fighting or any quarrelling, self control at all times or if not, over the side on a rope into the river for a cooler of a ducking. If you had bad feelings against anyone, you kept it under your collar and waited 'till 'Quarter Staff' day. No quarter asked or given, it was up to you alone to work of grudges and pent up dislikes and it cut both ways mind you! You were on your merit of take and give and god help the loser. No boxing or wrestling was allowed, this is why one hardly ever sees a sailor boxer or wrestler. To harbour a grudge is a dangerous thing aboard ship. Life and limb and ships crews safety can be at stake. Stay in your own Mess and keep your worries and troubles there. The Master-at-Arms, approached by the 'Leader of the Mess' is the one to see and sort out trouble. He is the father over his family, the one to set the course!

The moment 'Quarter Staff' starts you can soon tell if its grudge or not. Normally it is fast, nimble, two handed keen eyed manoeuvrability and very exciting too, to hear the staves meet 'click clack'. The Japanese Kendo is similar to it.

It's a pity there wasn't more of it in the schools of correction. There is a two cane sport, on in each hand, fast, furious and funny. They don't hurt unless you get a swipe across the kisser (which counts as a point). There was also quoits, skill and coordination of arm and eye, good sport. There was also hand over hand, no legs to be used, up 10 –15 feet over a spar and down the other side head down. Tug 'o War, skipping, through the Life buoy, Pyramids, Jig Dancing, Hornpipe, Cartwheels but the highlight was always 'Manning Aloft'. All hands aloft and positioned on spars, a beautiful sight, all in white No 1 ducks, barefooted, all the to pipe and then the Deck Muster, all hands 'shindy' down the lines. Marvellous, 128 hands slither down to muster in two ranks, Port and Starboard to stand at attention, stock still, only the chests heaving sucking in air. How long did it take on this occasion? From Pennant point to Muster point on the pipe, just 40 seconds!

'Ships crew mustered sir!'

'Ready for stations sir'

Boson 'fell in' aft of the line, the Coxswain opposite. They walked slowly, majestically with swords drawn, left hands holding scabbards, along the Port line, turned and walked back at the rear, viewing keenly the statues that were the crew, erect and unmoving. Then along the Starboard watch and seeming pleased the Captain said;

'Good show Lads'

For a 'Truant' ship we could more than hold our Quarter deck to the Warspite and Arethussa and many a good lad was made on her, a credit to HM Navy. I wonder, as I write now, how many are still alive like me and remember cocoa and hard tack, oakum picking, over the rope holy stoning; not many I'm afraid, most having attended the 'Last Muster' at six bells or 8 bells (sling hammock). I still hear the echo 'Look lively lads', but life is like that, it goes too quickly.

After piping 'Stand down' we turned smartly as one and saluted the Quarter deck and the White Ensign was lowered aft and furled. We were piped 'Break Away', to trot towards the gaping companion way and the Mess, each to their own in silence. 'Rooster' work came once every seventh week, responsible for fetching and carrying for the rest of the Mess for a one week period. The Mess leader, promoted to Able Seaman First Class, was responsible for all about the Mess, but we worked as a team. The Rooster 'Piggy' of the Mess would trot to the galley, take up Mess positions, 1 to 16, draw ships rations for eight and trot back, timed to the second. Eager hungry mouths would be chewing, clean rosy faces aglow with life. Rostered 'Skivs' would wash basins in a Dixie, eager hands wiping and stowing away. Decks were swabbed with mops and Boson would pipe 1 bell. One man from each mess would stand and report;
'All stowed Boson'

We sat, with both hands palm upwards on the table
and stow the tables as he passed. We would then
stow the forms and were ready for one hours night
school, piped at 2 bells. Then, the rest of the
evening was our own unless you were a defaulter.
Later Boson would pipe 'Sling hammocks' quickly
done and it was swing up and into the canvas to lay
snug and warm watching the lamp singing and
soon sleep would come. Sweet undisturbed sleep
in the silence, to be awakened by a tap on the side
of the hammock and;
    'Show a leg there, look lively Lad'
If you weren't out and on your feet in your night
flannel 'quick and lively like' you just got cut
down! That's all, no second telling! Still in your
flannel you had to reef (six and a half turns) with
the tie lashing line and tidily stow it, all in under
15 seconds. Mess by Mess you went to ablutions,
starkers, to sluice in cold water from 'Crown to
Keel', a quick wipe and trot back to the Mess to
get dressed ready for P.T. Cocoa would be waiting
for you, fetched by the Rooster. P.T. was 40
minutes or an hour, up aloft, round the deck, over
the Foc'sle and than 8 bells clanged and 128
hungry lads were ready for breakfast. Chunks of
fresh baked bread, a generous slice of fried pork
and fried potatoes and a basin of skilly and cocoa.
It Rarely altered though sometimes at tea we
would have haddock, cod, whiting or kippers. On
Sundays we had beef or mutton for dinner, ships
cake of sultanas, currents and peel and not

surprisingly not a morsel went over the side or in the Brock tub. Food wholesome food and plenty of it, and we benefited from it. Very rarely was anyone on a 'Blue Sheet'(sick report). The doctor had what we called a real 'Turkey time' of it, with hardly any work to do. Sometimes we had brawn on a Friday or Saturday. Saturday was our 'wash, mend and make do' day. The lines on deck were a wonderful sight at that time, as each article was 'clued' to the line. In the Foc'sle was a drying room for the winter months, heated by a Tortoise slow burning stove, it was like a Turkish bath in there, scant and bare except for the lines forming lanes the length of the room. The deck was snow white, as were all decks and each Mess had its own lane for hanging clothes. Saturday afternoon was piped 'Liberty Boat' for those eligible, Port watch one week and Starboard the next. One had to wait twelve months before being allowed liberty ashore to play football or netball.

On my third visit ashore I was off! The call of home was too strong to resist. I was never caught again, I have often thought of those days, my 'getting by' days, and again lays a story worth the telling.

Tell me reader, isn't there something missing in my story? Yes! What happened to Monkey?. As I wrote earlier, it was a toss up whether I'd be sent to the Mount Edgecome or the Cornwall. It must have come down 'tails' for me, Monkey got heads and was sent instead (as I was to find out years after when I met him in Mesopotamia (1924). I was to assume another character as my cover for the next three years 'till 1915. It was of no use going 'home' to 27 Croydon Road, there was nobody there. I knew that I had to change my togs so I nicked an overcoat in Grays Thurrock. The overcoat covered my jumper and hid the blue band of my flannel vest, which would have been a dead give away. I 'won' a couple of shirts off of a line in Romford and then a coat from a shop, which was simply begging to be taken! I made my way to Ingatestone, on to the Colchester-Chelmsford road, telling the sorry story to who ever would listen. I would cadge a feed and sleep wherever night found me. Eventually I arrived in Chelmsford, the wireless station and houses were being built there. I got an insurance card from the Post Office for the asking and got a job as tea boy to the labourers, sleeping in the tea hut. I was paid one shilling a day and a whip round at the weekends. All in all about eight shillings a week, fourpence of this was stopped

for an insurance stamp. I got by.. Christmas I spent at the 'Gangers home', after a short time the job petered out and I went to Lowestoft, getting a lift via Norwich in the brickies van by stages, Clacton-Wharton-Southwold then Lowestoft. The money that I had saved I kept in my 'blow-belt', a flannel belt round my tummy, it stood me in good stead. I slept in the seamen's mission, telling the tale of how I was waiting for my Dad to come home and he'd take me then. Meals at tuppence for breakfast, thruppence for dinner, tuppence for tea and for just seven pence a day lived like a lords son! Now, I love bloaters, or the next best thing, brown juicy kippers or skate and these were always given for the asking. I kept the mission going on them, but what I really wanted was to get on a sailing barge! One turned up in the shape of the Lord Warden, a G.W.Goldsmith craft, tied up at the pier and the Skipper came into the mission carrying a white linen duffle bag. Ostensibly to get some victuals and he got chatting to Superintendent Wiggins. Looking in my direction he beckoned me over and asked how would I like a berth with him as Cabin boy 3rd Hand. My pleasure must have show with the eagerness on my face. They shook hands and my new Skipper, Mr. Hill went out. The Super took me to his office to take down details in case 'Dad' (God bless him) turned up so he would know where to find me. Shortly, Skipper came back and we went to the barge. She was bound for Yarmouth and Grimsby with Portland stone for the harbours there. That then, by the grace of God, was how I became a sea/freshwater sailor. With my knowledge of my training I was a Godsend to him and he, in turn, a very loveable, kind and generous man, became my 2nd father. I stayed aboard the Lord Warden (a hundred tonner fore jib and stay sail craft – easy to

handle, lovely to sail), I was paid four shillings and
sixpence a week, got all my grub and clobber,
oilskins and jerseys 'till war was declared in
August 1914 (I was not quite 13 years of age).
Skipper was Royal Naval Reserve and was called
up, we were in Sheerness at the time, just back
from the Isle of Wight with a hold full of granite
chippings. I went with him to Chatham dockyard
and when he saw me crying he held me and kissed
me saying;

    'I'll be back soon son!'
and with that I lost (except Grand dad and Mum),
he finest friend a youngster could have.

Chapter Seven

The Monkey and the Sailing Barge

Today the waterways are coming back into their own and people are gaining a new relaxation by using them. Draw a line from Hull in the East to Liverpool in the West and a series of criss cross lines to run South East and West from Manchester, Stoke, right down to the River Thames and running North from the Severn and Avon and you could safely say you are drawing the veins of the 17th 18th 19th and 20th century trade life lines of these era's. Some are still workable and in existence, the Grand Union, Regents, London to the 'Black Country' runs. For these a very special barge was built, the Monkey barge, an apt name for such a craft! One had to be of monkey adroitness to walk the gunwale of one as one had only a matter of inches to manoeuvre on. They were family house craft and the home of the bargee, his wife and children, who lived and died on them. They were very ornately dressed in brass and copper decorations and kept spic and span, it must have been a hard competitive life for them. Like most things of pre 1914 they were to become uneconomic and so became redundant. Such is the modern age. Yet attempts are being made to use these canals again. To that I'd say YES, by all means. But the slog will have gone. The diesel engine and propeller will have taken over and the steady way of getting from place to place gone forever. I unfortunately was never to know this means of waterway and I regret at not being able to experience this life. Britain is much the poorer by losing these lovely little craft and the people who worked them. Such is greed and the desire for a 'Quick Penny'. Yet we may yet recapture the tranquillity of those bygone days. It goes as a very fitting compliment to the builders of these canals. Behind them they have left a monument and a heritage for the future generations. May they yet again prosper. Getting on board of craft of the same calling I would be more at home with the sailing barge that was to be a heritage too. It is commemorated every year by a race of skill in its honour, like the Doggett Coat and Badge Race. When I state skill, I mean exactly that, when every trick of the tide and elements had to be known. 'Tis true, the saying, 'You cannot bluff the waves and the wind' (well, not too often). Manned by 'Skippers' who from boy and man had served their apprenticeships to life's end, learning the hard way to hold in respect the lessons taught. Fathers taught sons, sons taught their sons and oft times they could trace their genealogy back 300 years of sailing barges. You could never hurry the tide or the wind and had to use them when they set the 'terms' which state clearly 'Time and Tide waits for no man'. In those days (when there were no weather forecasts), skill and brawn were used in order to make the destination using time, tide and wind to the fullest advantage. To help in all of this was the skill of the barge builders, once again these were 'Family concerns', who gave of their workmanship and craft to not only uphold their name for quality, but to make sure all demands for competent handling could be relied on. From the Lateen sail and oar for rudder (or prow guidance) there developed as we know it now, the 'Morning Cloud', the 'Shamrock' and the 'Liberty Class', those slim, strong greyhounds. All of these a far cry from the 'Humper' we knew, but the 'Humper' was built for work, weather and water and fulfilled those requirements asking only for care in return. Not only care was given, but love also, real human love, right from the common and garden 'Sally Ann' right up to 'Princess May' class. Each one nursed and cared for by a loving mind, as though it were Wife or Daughter. The 'Lord Warden' was one of these. Skipper Mr. Hill, like a true 'Waterman' of Suffolk/Norfolk breed (of the old Norsemen tradition) was all about the boat! He'd talk to her, coax her, ask her 'What's wrong lass?'. At first I thought this strange, hearing him at the wheel, talking! But as he would say 'Er be a funny yen at toimes and she likes a word or two now'n agin' like y'see?'. I didn't see for a long time. 'They be like a woman or a horse, they like their head, now'n agin like, they are easier to 'andle thata way and give we'r a chuckle doan ye lass?' But as I have said, he was a very loveable natured man. Yet I've seen the fury come out in him at times, when for instance a fellow struck a Swan Vista match on the foremast. He grabbed this boyo in those capable hands and shook him like a terrier would a cat! 'Doan 'e ever do that agin to her , now get ashore with yer', and literally lifted him, by the arse of his trousers and collar, over the side. Another example, the time a guy lifted the hatch cover and slung in on the deck. Skip picked up said hatch cover in one hand and hit the merchant a 'sender' with it and with his other hand a swipe as a 'make weight' 'Teach 'e to have care of a lady's dress in future!'

He would be addressed, as demanded, Mr. Hill and to hear dockers say 'Yes Mr. Hill' was something to hear. Any backchat and that capable hand would travel fast and sore. 'Teach 'e to have respect from now on'.

The 'Lord Warden' was always spic and span and Bristol fashion. I've know him to climb aloft to Pennant Point, bring the Green with Gold triangular pennant down, wash it, iron it with the old fashioned iron and take it back up, come down on deck, look up and look pleased as it fluttered.

He would rub his hands and say 'Doan 'e look better for it son?' he would, while he was up there, inspect the Foresail an mast, pulley's and lines meticulously not hurrying at all. He would oil the pulley's with a little can he always stowed up there 'tween the foremast and main mast. The foresail wire runner was his next visit (running from Jib to Jack point) in case of loose wire strands ('It could go son, when we need it most'). Any and everything on deck had a full 'Masters inspection' and, with my Cornwall training, which came in very handy to him now, was helpful to keep him happy and have peace of mind. Everything moveable was greased and oiled, she made for easier handling that way.

So, let's start an inspection shall we. Going forward up to the Fore Jib, see that the golden varnish is alright, to the pulley, a drop of oil on it until smoothly running at a touch of a finger. Check the lines are intact, step down, brackets and braces, no sign of rust and secure the sails, stowage locker, putting a drop of oil on the hinges. Ensure the sails are nicely stowed and lashed and ready for instant use. Look at the 'Devils eye' where the chain holding the anchor was to make sure it was clear and free, trace the chain to the windlass, grease, oil and mark for painting if required. Inspect Fore hatch covers and go down into Foc'sle and inspect there. Take tally on gear, such as oil for pumps, spares etc. noting any shortages.

Check the riding light fastened at the back of the mid mast (this was used at night at anchor to warn other craft, a round lamp some 18 inches in diameter which could easily be seen from main brace). One of my daily jobs was to keep this filled, trimmed and clean and to light it up at dusk. The next one on 'Port Saddle' was a big half round copper one with a red magnifying glass, a lift out bar moved outwards and it was free to take out and inspect. Over to Starboard, the same with that, a green one. Amidships now, the small winch to hoist the M'sheet and F'sail ropes and lines nicely furled and laid ready to run at a touch along gunwale. A look down the hold was invited and done. Then stepping over the 'Boom Bar', a round solid beam of 18 inches diameter which ran from Port to Starboard. Along this ran a solid one and a half inch ring on which, when sailing, the main sheet was hooked so that when tacking it carried the sheet in which ever way it was required. Our next job was to connect up the line on the 'Side Vanes' or 'Wings' which were round edged and triangular flaps of iron bound solid wood of some 4 to 6 inches and were used to give aid to steerage when needed. It was very clever how much purchase could be brought to bear when running light with no cargo or running with the tide against the wind. Even when loaded it would, in a strong wind, help keep the barge stabilised. In fact you could say they were mobile stabilisers. The stronger the wind the lower they were dropped.

The sails of a barge, in heavy canvas, were red, the Jibs and Fore Topsails white, which gave a very nice effect. All lines were manila and hemp. A look at the Mizzen Mast and the furled sheets, pulley's and lines were gone over and a glance into the white painted fresh water tank followed. Now the most important part – the Steering Chain and the shackles to the wheel. These were meticulously gone over, inch by inch. These were in fact the most valuable assets on board. Many a craft has been lost because of lack of supervision. The Binnacle came in for its share, great care was taken here, Mr. Hill would 'square inch' all over, sometimes even twice, to make sure that nothing could go wrong, yet it was housed as secure as the Bank of England and nothing, it seemed, could go wrong! Yet Skipper knew of cases where it had so there! Nothing for it but to make sure and I'd back my life on his estimation of things (I oft times wondered if he had tested me in the past and, if so, how and when?). How many times in his casual questions had he 'probed' out of me the truth and never been lacking in getting it. How so patient he was with me, yet I know not that I ever gave him a moment of doubt or brought a frown to his forehead, I was always 'Son'. I could have given myself away when he kissed me 'Bye Son' but let's not dwell on that now. Below, lifting our leg over the step cover and descending into the cabin, six steps down and we were in a small 8 x 10 x 6 foot room. On the Port side a small bed berth 2

foot 6 inches wide, 6 foot long and 2 inches high,
just enough room to snuggle into, it was so comfy.
There were 3 of these, Port, Aft and Starboard.
Skip had Port, I had Starboard and Aft was empty
(for a 'Mate' as he would be known if aboard). In
the centre was a small 2 x 4 foot table which
hooked into two latches and had a dropping leg
which bedded into a small hole in the floor and
could be taken down and stowed on the side. A
locker with a hinged lid ran all around the room on
which we sat. About 12 inches in width it was used
for coal for the fire and our odds and ends. Pretty
dinky really, there were 4 little cupboards in which
our crocks and food were kept and a swinging
hanging safety oil lamp hung from the centre
below the skylight. The chief feature was the little
dinky stove/oven built like the Kitchener on a
smaller scale. There was always a copper kettle
singing its little heart out, a rack above it to dry
and air your damp clothes. It was so roomy yet
compact, you could boil, fry roast, cook anything
in record time on it. You have to see one to believe
it could be done. It was never allowed to go out
Summer or winter, controlled by a damper and
funnelled by a small stack pipe. It was easily
cleaned and was never any bother. Our 'wants'
books and papers (of which I couldn't read
anyhow), were on tap at the missions. The
groceries, when ashore, were collected in a white
bag, potatoes, onions, cabbage all were kept on
deck in a locker. Food was always well stocked,

bread had to last us but, kept in a semi damp cloth, was always fresh tasting. But (of course) it was real bread then, Farm baked with condensed milk. So there was nothing we ever wanted for, absolutely nothing! Mr. Hill hardly ever smoked (I didn't) and he never drank beer but did like a cup of toddy Rum now and again. Careful to the nearest farthing we sometimes went weeks without pay but, when my money would be given to me (and the habit has stayed with me since), I would have £1 by me as it was always handy to have some money close by. When we berthed, as often happened, we loaded up for mobs for the deck, I'd make 'em up (and still do so long as I have a base). This tickled him when I first did it, on of the things that would have given me away, my use of the palm pad. Another, the way I handled a line or rope 'You have been ship trained, I can see that, where?' He know of Grand dad and Dad and the Cornwall and how I came to be in the mission when we walked in. 'You are a natural' he would say and chuckle. I'd darn his socks or Guernsey and all his buttons and odds and ends. I would help repair the sails as we lay at anchor. Sunny days and sea breezes and when, from Grimsby, Yarmouth to the Thames, round the flats, Goodwins to Ryde on the Isle of Wight, I would have my turn at the wheel and be shown how to lay a point, veer on to another and hold it 'till the last moment. Lay over a point or to port, those days, (like the song 'We thought would never end') sadly did! Such is fickle destiny, ours never to own or be master of. Yet, may I state in conclusion, the Lord Warden and Mr. Hill were among the happiest days of my life and it is a life I would recommend to any lad desirous of learning sea craft, it satisfied me . Instead of borstal for correction a few tall masted craft racing round the Hebrides or the Dogger Bank would change 'em or drown 'em. If that wasn't enough, run 'em over the 'Western' to St. Johns, Newfoundland, aye, it would either make 'em or break 'em.

Thank you for being so patient with me and please do forgive the handwriting

Your loving dad

Chapter Eight

Home and Away

I found the Hornet, a stumpy masted barge of
60 tonnes, of Goldsmiths fleet (the Lord Warden
being commandeered for ammunition carrying to
Calais via the Woolich Arsenal in Erith Rands
Reach). I was oft to see it laying with riding lights,
drab and unpainted, not at all the spruce lord it
once was. I often passed the Cornwall and kid like,
hid myself in the cabin in case I would be spotted.
We carried all sorts of cargo up and down the river
from Battersea, Prices Candle Works, working the
bridges being under tow of the Union Lighterage
and Tug Company, with the tug showing the
owners colours of red, yellow and green bands
round the funnel. It as easy work really and I
learned every reach from Battersea to Sea Reach
off by heart. I learned to lay the race tides, of the
pulls in the twisting river bends. I knew all the
wharf frontages and every inch of the river from
Prices to Tillbury, both sides of the river. The river
Medway too! In 1915 I came ashore when we were
up Dartford Creek with a load of paper for the

cartridge mills, which served the woolwich Arsenal. I 'slung my hook' ashore, leaving my dunnage behind and, with the readies (cash) in my blow belt, jumped on a train from Craford to Fenchurch Street. The urge of wanting to be back in my home town strong within me. So, dear reader, ends another chapter of my memories and adventures of childhood. I was 14 years of age and fit to be independent and work for my own living without any fear of being caught and taken back!

All I was concerned with was to get home again. This took dominant precedence in my mind. On the train, which all seemed so strange compared to the isolated quietness of the barge Hornet seemed bewildering as it 'chickeree'd' up the line stopping at every station Belvedere-Woolwich-Greenwich-Deptford-New Cross to take the branch line to Loughboro' Junction and then Vauxhall to Fenchurch Street, crossing the river. People got on and off at the stations and when we drew into Fenchurch Street it was almost empty, but the platforms weren't. As we pulled in the platforms were crowded with sailors, sweethearts and wives and a fair number of civvy chaps all bound for Chatham navy works. There was a rush for seats and it was quite a job to push through them and, not being used to it, I was glad to get out to the bus which was to take me home. Home? What? I had nowhere to go and it wasn't going to be another kip house adventure for me! I wasn't a bona-fide sailor who could get into one of the missions. The Salvation Army asked too many questions and I didn't want to chance getting caught again. But where was I to go then? I know! As a bright spark of an idea struck me.

'Fares please' said a voice, I asked for one to Poplar, I paid the tuppence and 'Ping' I was going to Uuncle Stormy's or Masty's house to see what I could do from there. 'Upper Street North' said the voice and I landed on the curb with uncle Stormy's house facing me. I crossed over and knocked on the brass knocker and Auntie Polly appeared at the door. For a second or two she looked at my smiling face and then the penny dropped. 'Mick? Why bless my soul! Come in, come in' and into the little passage that let into the back kitchen I knew so well. Uncle Stormy and his two kids, a big boy and girl, were sitting at the table. Auntie close behind me. Uncle Stormy's eyes nearly popped out of his head, he looked and said;
'Gawd strike me pink – young Mick' (so I couldn't have changed that much facially). Herbert and Lillian, the terrible two, were grinning. Auntie made a pot of tea and over this I told them the layout of the last four years. Uncle and Auntie, all ears, asked if this was the truth I was telling them and I told them 'Yes, nothing but the truth'. I got to the point and told them I had no where to go and could they help me. Uncle Stormy told me I could bunk down on the sofa and that he would get me

fixed up in a day or two. Dear Uncle kept on chuckling to himself. Auntie told me about Mum (who was in Goodmayes at this time) and of the rest of the family and sent for Uncle Masty to come. It was lateish and he was half cut as he walked it, sized me up and said;

'He has filled out eh Stormy'

Stormy outlined the picture and Masty said;

'Why, Esther will have him I'm sure, she liked her little Mick'. To me he said;

'You know Auntie Esther Mick,
and to Auntie Polly; 'Poll, it's a bit late now but Ill get Milly to run over tomorrow and tell her'.

Yes, I was home again with my kin folk once more. We had a fish and 'tater supper and a pot of stout for Auntie Polly and some beer in a big jug for Uncles Masty and Stormy. Tea for us youngsters (incidentally, the parrot kept chiming in and squatted on top of the cage, head cocked) 'Still got him for you Mick' chuckled Uncle Stormy. We talked, or rather I had to answer a lot of questions as the occasion called for. Masty said;

'Bet they're bleedin' glad to see the back of you' and to Uncle Stormy;

'Been a bit of a sod in his time eh? This is going to tickle Mill when I tell her'.

A bed was made for me on the sofa and soon I was asleep, fast off! In the morning the terrible two went off to school and Uncle had gone to work. Auntie cooked some rashers and fried slices and later on a knock on the street door and Aunties Milly and Esther walked in.

'Poor little sod, that Sarah wants blinding, the 'ard 'earted cow she does! Wait 'till I clap eyes on her. Never mind Mick, you can stay with Auntie Esther, she'll look after you, poor little sod'.
Had Sarah or Mr. Dora walked in that moment they would have been lynched! Auntie Poll had been out and got some faggots and peas pudding for dinner. They were a rough and ready, warm hearted lot. More stout was consumed to keep the 'pot boiling' and come about 3pm the 'must be going' time was at hand for Auntie Esther and I. Kisses all round and we were seen onto the bus. So, Mick rode into Canning Town with a home to go to (78 Edward Street) and love and security with it! I was given real love there, though the first two years were unsettled ones. I was in and out of jobs until I joined H&W Nelsons Line and went to sea, later to go on Liverpool and HM Eagle and war service. Yes dear reader, there is so much to tell of those years from 1909-11-15-19-26 and onwards. Why, I'd be kept busy writing my 2002 tales for years to come and all in truth and facts. I still ask myself 'what is it all in aid of? What is the purpose of it all? What is the answer?.

How proud the day was, when, in my navy uniform I went to Goodmayes to visit my dear Mum. Her baby, her 'darlint 'o bhoy Mick.' Was it a wise thing to do? Did I make her happy and content or did I cause tears and sorrow and soul searing memories? I left a photo of myself and a load of goodies and money for her' but not being able (because I couldn't then) to write, silence and memories for all those long years; but Mum dear, I often thought and cried for you. I was taken too suddenly (or you were from me) and in my mind I go to the East London Cemetery where you lay, in the family grave keeping Dad, Grand dad and Grand mama company. Peace my love.

It is said it is not a wise thing to do, to go back into the mists of the past and rake over the ashes and ruins. Be that as it may, we all harbour in our minds memories and I think it is a sensible thing to do, to air them now and again and if tears are wont to fall and you cry, make sure that you cry alone as the song says. Even though your heart be aching and it feels as thought its breaking, cover it up with a smile (and so live a lie) It seems like I start this letter in despondency and if I'm not careful will end it in a sad mood. Well, sleep is not far away and that will cure that. My Grand daughter gets married today and so my son won't be here to visit so sleep is the best way out. I have anticipated that you would want this chapter so I have written it for you.

Chapter Nine

A Lad who got by
Part One

Waving goodbye to Aunties Milly and Polly, we (Auntie Esther and I) started off on our journey. Let me describe the LGOC bus of that day. Solid tyred and a real falting bone shaker with caned seas of two decks, inside to hold 14 and the top deck (which was open) a further 16. When it rained there was a black apron to cover your legs. There were two services, No. 15 – East Ham town hall to Ladbrokes Grove and No. 40 – Upton Park to the Elephant and Castle. When you wanted to get off you just pulled the overhead cable and you stopped, there and then, anywhere you wished (no forced stops as there are today). The fare was 1 penny for Auntie and a halfpenny for me. Along East India Dock Road through Poplar onto Canning Town Iron Bridge and down the Barking Road (incidentally, excepting Romford Road, the longest straight road in East London). At Croydon road, or rather, Braemar Road, Auntie pulled the cord and we got off. I had been feasting my eyes on a scene I

hadn't seen for nigh on 4 years, all of which I knew
off by heart and all of which I can still journey
when I want to. Auntie and I crossed over by the
corner Eel and Pie shop as she had to get
something in for tea (she remembered I loved
bloaters and so got 2 big ones for a penny 'hapenny
a piece) a piece of skate for herself and two pieces
of Newfoundland cod (tuppence) for Frankie's tea.
We went into Liptons for 6 eggs for the girls tea, a
large cottage loaf (tuppence farthing). Then we
went down Ingal Road into Edward Street and I
was soon indoors. By now it was just getting dark,
the gas mantled street lights were being lighted by
a man on a bike who carried a lighter iron, a brass
pole which he poked through a small trap door
pushing a lever up to turn the gas on (it took but a
second for the whole operation). It gave a fair light
too. We went through the small passage, past the
front room, past the small stove which led to our
bedrooms and into the kitchen. The Kitchener was
alight and pulling the damper lever open the fire
was soon well away. Auntie used waxed paper to
light the gas and put the bloaters in the grid iron,
the cod in milk in the oven. The kettle was singing,
a whist of steam coming from its spout. A gallon
enamel teapot was filled, bread cut and by now
Frank (our lodger of whom I will tell you) came
downstairs from his back room. May and Lilly
would soon be home from their waitressing jobs. A
clean spotless tablecloth was spread on the table
and tea was ready. In this tiny snug room, with its

sofa and four chairs grace was said and we tucked in to a lovely homely tea. So different from my Cornwall, Union and barge life. It was more like being at home at 27 or at Grand dads. It seemed as though I had come home once more.

Auntie was widowed with 3 girls, Esther, who was married, May who was about to marry and Lilly who was engaged. Frank Gibson was Uncle Herbert's ships chum, thin and asthmatic (poor soul). I realise now, Frank, what you went through and this is how it came about. Uncle Herbert (Dads brother) was, like the rest of the family, a 'Tar', working the whalers out of Hamburg in the summer and out of Fleetwood in the winter. It paid good money and he was part owner of the Codder (a whaler). On one trip Frank and Uncle were wrecked of St. Johns, only 3 were saved, Frank being one of them, but the cold days in the lifeboat took its toll and he never got better, which left him as an asthmatic wreck. He died in 1922. Frank was on a pension of 8 shillings a week and Auntie (who was sort of 'well off') charged him 6 shillings a week for his board and lodgings and Frank was always grateful and always bought a quarter of peardrops (1 penny) and a quarter of stick jaw (cocoanut toffee) for the house. H would have a half pint every day and always saw to it that there was tuppence on the mantle piece for the gas. All cooking was done on the Kitchener stove which Frank kept stoked up. Coal was elevenpence halfpenny a hundredweight and a hundredweight would last a week with no stinting. It was into this atmosphere of love and care I bedded down that night in March 1915.

I had a couple of days at home, getting the feel of it. The 12 pounds I had in my blow belt, in ten shilling notes (green Bradbury's as they were known then), I gave to Auntie to look after for me. I had no use for it. She bought me some clothes, shirts, socks, two pairs of shoes, one pair of boots, long trousers and a coat. I was togged out! Now, 12 pounds was a lot of money in those days and came in handy when short times were to come, although shortages and the inch of the war hadn't hit us yet. The Lusitania had been sunk, the Zeppelins were to be seen in the searchlights at night. The air raid warning was by Police, racing round the streets on bicycle ringing bells, but no one took any notice of them! No lights went out, shops kept open, life went on as usual. On a fine summers night in June, Lieutenant Warneford attacked one over Cuffleyand sent it blazing down, which could be seen for miles, great excitement!

On my trips into Edward Street on my first day back, I met some of the boys I knew at school. The news of 'Mickey' Jennings being back was soon being passed from boy to boy and their mums and from there to their neighbours, and soon, all knew of the return of 'Mick'. When I walked up the street, bounded by Ingall Road at one end and Cross Street/Star Lane at the other, people would come to their doors and shout hello to me along with comments about how well I looked and how much I had grown. So, at this point let me introduce you to them. At Nr. 72, the corner Rag Shop, Mr. Reid, at 74, Mrs Regan, 76, Mrs Corpse, 78, Isterly, 80, Mrs Roberts, 82/84, Mrs Clarke, 86, Mrs Forfar, 88, Mrs Hannigan, 90, well, I never knew them? On the opposite side, 91, Mrs Offer, 89, Mrs Mayby, 87, Mr Marriott, 85 Mrs Hodgson, numbers 83 and 81 escape me and finally 79, Mrs Crow. Next to that in Star Lane was a warehouse and then the 'Bug Flea Cockroach' factory that made sailors beds out of coir horse hair flock. (Seamen and Stokers could buy these 'lay ons' for anywhere between one shilling and half a crown. Imagine though, what they were like because they were burnt after a trip, being alive with vermin, although some found their way back into circulation again (especially the horse hair ones, used to stuff chair seats and sofa's). The 'bug' could be found in nigh on every house in the dockland, coming originally from this source.

A sailors dunnage could bring them ashore and cockroaches in the boxes and sea chests. Lice and fleas came to, mostly from the East India boats and sailors homes, to be spread all over. The first job on coming home from a trip was to burn the gear you were wearing or boil in the copper in carbolic the gear you would take on your next trip. Keating powder was always a must, both in the home and on board. In this flea/bug of a factory there was a sulphur room for the fumigation of the material used in beds but I don't think for one moment though that it stopped it. In No. 78 we had a half gallon hand spray with Jeyes 'special' disinfectant with a scented smell which was used at the first sign of a bite or bug and we kept clean and clear of them! Every Saturday all beds, rooms, walls and corners got a spray, wanted or not, Auntie saw to that and Frank made that his job. The Jeyes factory was in West Ham Lane and I was to work there and we never did go short of 'juice' (and scented moth blocks too). I was accepted by the boys and the parents and had many happy months. My first job was to help in Barhams Yard, going to Spitafeilds or Covent Garden for fruit and vegetables, for seven shilling and sixpence a week. It was a dead end job with no excitement and, to 'keep in with the boys' I would leave the yard gates open while I went into the shop and they (naturally) helped themselves and so I got the sack for being careless. I soon found another job as a van boy with Coombes, who delivered Jams, sugar and jars of sweets to outlying small country shops. It was easy work but monotonous. My next job was driving a big white mare for Hoopers (coal merchants) of Beeton Road, going to Woolwich and loading up glass sand for the Canning Town glass works. (Can you imagine me Dad, driving the big horse and van proudly down Edward Street and pulling up in front of 78!). I took a few of the boys to Woolwich and back to the glass works and Hooper, the old man, saw me and yes, you guessed it, I got the 'bullet'. I then went to Goodacre's (William Goodacre and Sons Ltd) in Butchers Road Custom House employed burning the coir coconut clippings in a furnace outside the boiler house. If I cleared the lot by Saturday noon, I got an extra half a crown. So, once, I set light to the whole lot and nearly burnt the factory down and naturally enough, there was another job I got paid off from! Scouting around the docks I found very lucrative job as 'beer boy' to Cory's coal humpers. Ships in those days were coaled by gangs working from barges laid alongside ships in the docks by means of baskets and jenny wheels operated by gangs of men loading them with coal for the voyages. It was all tonnage and piece work, real hard. There were no tea breaks nor coffee shops in those days, no dinner breaks, one worked on a job straight through. My job was to nip to the tavern and supply the gangers with their beer. A penny on the bottle was my perk, plus tupppence or thruppence a day from the gang. I was kept pretty busy and if I was given sixpence I would give the chappie his change and be honest. I was trusted and well liked, favoured you may say. I did well and everything I earned I gave to Auntie for food. I'd share the coal workers food and never went hungry. Pubs being open all day, I'd get a dozen or so bottles filled in the Custom House or Tidal Basin Taverns in the jug and bottle off sales bar. Each bottle was sealed with a sticky label (the law was such then) and in a News of the World canvas bag I would have my first 'issue' of beer ready! Knowing what berth the next ship had, by 9am I would be on my second trip. I made a mint on that job and it was the longest shoreman job I had held so far. The ships got fewer and fewer though and the 'Coalies' less and less and so it petered out for me. 'Jerry', by his torpedoing of ships was leaving his mark! Berths stood empty, food was now getting scare too. Where once there were pickings for the taking it slowly closed down. I got a job soap making in John Knights in Sivertown. I got fed up with that, hour after hour bumping out tablets of soap – ugh. Then I went to Nucoline's making margarine (night work, and Sunday nights at that!) which I never did take to, though we were never short of margarine. I was also able to get lots of nuts from which it was made by presses. The old parrot never did go short while I was there. I'd load my pockets up and bring them home and go over to Uncle Stormy's (and always with a bottle of stout and best stingo in each hand), and hand of a loaded nut bag for polly. That bird knew my voice too and her constant 'Hullo, hullo, hullo, Polly wants to cry' always welcomed me. I'd take sweets and odds ad ends too. I always think back of how good they were to me. May and Lilly had got married, Lilly went to Tooting Beck to live and May lived in Oak Crescent. Still the loner, I went to Woolwich Arsenal to work in the light machine shop, night work again. This time on bonus work along with Babs Hudson, Tommy Offer, Jack Crowe and Jim Clarke and so I had company. There was no such thing as canteens in those days, you took your dinner in a bowl or pie dish, put it in a square oven at meal times and took it out piping hot. You made tea in a beer can from a boiler, your tea, sugar and condensed milk you took in a Colemans mustard tin. You worked 12 hour shifts and were kept at it non stop. If you wanted to earn money and to get two pounds or two pounds ten shillings you really put all you had into it. Your expenses: Insurance fourpence, one shilling a week bus fare (tuppenny workman's return from Canning Town station to North Woolwich, a trip across the river on the free ferry, a walk up Beresford Road into the square) and into you factory section. For twelve hours a prisoner, no roaming around the arsenal. In the morning the bell went and we trooped out. One could be tapped on the shoulder to go back inside to be searched and rubbed down. The monotony of the dead end jobs, none, with the exception of the 'beer job' I liked and was still restless for something 'over the horizon'. Jobs for lads were ten a penny there was no excitement in any of them. In the paper every day were lists of killed and missing, endless columns of them. Christmas came and went. After a spell in the King George V docks, Auntie saw I was unsettled, though, bless her, she seemed to understand. In the 'kitty' there was 44 pounds, so there was no worry there and I was always able to forage for any shortages there may have been in the cupboard. Slowly but surely thing were getting short but, knowing my way round and by devious means I managed to keep supplies going. All this Auntie understood and made allowances for. 'Mick' could do no wrong, not in her eyes anyway. I was always truthful to her, still keen of eye and fleet of foot, plus a few more years of experience at 'getting by'. I was well adapted to my environment and there was plenty of room to get about in and no restrictions, it sort of satisfied me in a small way. The roaming nature inside of me, I'd go and do just how the day found me in mood and there was always the odd way to add a penny or sixpence or a shilling. A feed in a coffee shop took care of the food side. While you had cash in your pocket you could always get what was wanted. I've cut some capers to get a coin, yet by a close boundary margin kept on the right side of the law.

My new hunting ground was Poplar, East India Docks, west India Docks and Millwall Docks, brand spanking unknown and untouched ground! China town, Limehouse, Cubitt town, Wapping, London Docks and St. Katherine Docks. I always told Auntie where I had been and emptied my pockets of coins and odds and ends and she would smile as long as I was safe and happy. Happy I was, free to do what I wanted, to go where I wanted too. The docks had an magnetic attraction for me, so much new to see, so many different ships to go aboard. New smells from all parts of the world and it was a lucky lucrative are for me. I ate very little at home but brought something home with me every day. Dear old Frank always treated me kindly, always giving me little tips which I was sensible enough to heed and take notice of. I am so glad I did. Lord Derby had his conscript bill passed and it was being put into effect. More women were to fill their places so vacancies at the docks were available. The ships were getting fewer and ships berths were easier to get but you had to be 16 before you could go to sea. You had to produce your birth certificate to prove it, unless you went as a Cabin boy or Galley boy and were vouchsafed for by a registered sailor who signed for your good character etc. As a little knowledge never did anyone any harm, and working on Franks tips, I was to learn the tricks off by heart and sometimes a little bluff. I would make it my business to offer - free if you like- to do little jobs on ships. Ships cooks would tell and show and then let me do jobs. This would be my teaching. Yet I'd get a couple of bob for helping out and a meal and perhaps a few extras. I also got a police pass authorising me to have them. I'd come out of the dockyard gates well britched and with a taster to take home. Frank was always a cheerful listener, enjoying my stories of what happened today on board S.S. so and so and Auntie would smile and nod. Frank would say 'It'll do you no harm to learn'. I looked my age, sturdy and well built, on the lines of a 'young bull'. Weekends were very lucrative for me, sometimes making a bomb! Seven and six, eight shillings even ten shillings, all hones too (surprisingly enough). It all went into the house kitty except say sixpence or eightpence spending money. A penny packed of Woodbines for Frank and a penny for his pint.

Auntie and I went to see Mama in Goodmayes, she was always pleased to see us. I very often was upset to the point of tears at leaving her and always got those feelings of hate for my sisters and their husbands. I've never managed to 'live it out' of my soul and I never will! Grand dad and Grand mama had already passed on and Hermit Road seemed like and empty, bleak street to me. On my side, I somehow still felt alone though these moods were soon got over in 'getting by'. Yet it was those moods which tempered the mind, to be bloody determined to prove Grand dad and Mum right 'A chip off the old block, he's a Mick alright Mary Ann!' and Mum, her wee mouth in a grim line would nod and kiss me.

I never went into a factory to work again. What I was doing suited me down to the ground. Pickings were good, easy and often and I had all the love I needed showered upon me at home in No. 78. It seemed that the last seven and a half years had been well worth going through and I didn't regret it. They had laid a foundation I was to find, they had been the making of me though I had yet to learn the lessons and experience that which was yet to come.

Auntie saw to it that I had a nice birthday, I felt so grown up and big, because I was sixteen now and lots of privileges of being sixteen were mine now, to exercise as I thought fit! I could go into a pub now, stand at the bar a call for a drink, which I did, taking Frank round to the Mann and Crossmans British Empire and treated him. I felt ten feet tall as I drank my shandy among men. I could buy cigarettes and smoke if I wished, a one penny packet of five Woodbines. I was no longer to be thought of as a boy, yes, it was a lovely birthday. I left Frank happy, Auntie and I went over to Poplar and a good time was had by all! I still had change out of the pound and Auntie was quite proud of me. The following Sunday we went to see Mum for the hours visit allowed (it was my special birthday request), and after getting back to 78 I got an awful feeling of restlessness and went down to 27 Croydon Road and stood outside for a while. I then retraced my steps back to 78 again and had tea, winkles, buttered toasted muffins and that cheered me up a little. It was a nice balmy warm night, still light 'till 8.30 and I went for a walk on my own, along the Barking Road to Canning Town. I came back to the Abbey Arms as Frank had said at the tea table that he would be in the

British Empire just after 7 and I found him there. We had an hour or so in there but I had said that we would be home by eight, and eight it was as we trooped in that snug cosy room. Esther May and Lily had been and gone so Auntie had not been lonely. At 9 o'clock we were in bed as I had to look for another session the Millwall Dock the next day. I must have dozed off when poor old Frank's chest started having one of its turns. I could hear his wheezing, coughing that dry cough asthmatics have. I went into him and asked him if I could help him, asked where his 'Potters' asthma cure bottle was and I lit the Prices night light candle in its tin lid. I went down and got his bottle full of steaming water and took it up and he held his head over the spout with the towel covering his head. This is what he wanted so badly, the inhaler (to such poor souls it is a life saver). I stayed with him and settled him 'till he dozed off and went back to bed and soon I was asleep until Auntie called me with a cup of tea (bless her!). I went to see how Frank was but he had already got up and was downstairs. He thanked me for the previous night. I was washed, dressed and out within half an hour, on my way to Millwall. A one penny bus to West India Dock Road and this is Limehouse, a ghetto of Chinese fame (I know the area well and could write lots of little stories of that area). There is little if anything left of it now and gone is a tradition unique in itself. Penny Fields and its teeming silk robes, pigtailed shuffling figures, its scent and perfumes, its mystery. Only Limehouse church is still there to remind us that we are in Limehouse. The opium dens may be gone but it still stays fresh in my 'Lads Memory'. Millwall is situated in an are known as 'The Isle of Dogs'. Sometime in the 1800's the Jennings family came from Glamorgan to settle there though doubtless there had been those on the trade masted sailing ships of the 1750's 'West Indies' and East India' men. Grand dad, there as a lad, spoke of Great Grand dad and the mutiny of Spithead and the Nore. He spoke of his Grand dad in Bristolian and Cardiff runs. Dad was born in the Isle of Dogs and married mum there. Actually the Isles were repair and boat building yards, serving St. Katherine, London, Millwall and West India docks. That has all gone too now. The firm McConachies was there but it was originally a warehouse of chandlers of ships stores, selling ropes and other gear. Everyone who lived in those little shacks was of the sea or river men. I have roved every inch of it (perhaps answering some hereditary call of my ancestors) searching for I know not what. Perhaps just a family memory which I never found. I had trod in the footsteps of this family, there is no doubt of that, I must have!

By now the pinch of the U boats was being felt, plus the lack of stevedores and Dockers to unload the big boats coming into the docks. Women were seen working now where men once were. Pickings still came and supplemented cash though, I made enough to clear the demands and I still had time on my hands to rove and roam. Times though, were slowly changing, imperceptibly, nut never the less changing. The Lascars and Blacks from the British-India Steam Navigation Company were not so prominent as they were. Where there had been life a quietness had come, unfortunately to stay as today remains only a nostalgic memory. I may not recognise it now, but if you took me there I would tell you what was there and could weave a story round it. What was to me a happy hunting ground has no doubt become a desert of memories. Such is life, for we move on ever changing. I took your Mum there once, before the second war, it was derelict then and Jerrys bombs finished it between 41 and 44, changed forever, on part of the East end that I knew!

I have no regret of those days, only a lot of happy carefree memories. I was not to know it then but the 'moving finger' was writing and soon, within days, life was to be altered for me. A New Zealand Steam Ship Company boat was sailing past Tilbury, bound for the Albert Dock and on board was Herbert, home after a round trip from Wellington NZ of 18 months! At about 4 o'clock on Wednesday afternoon he walked in (I was, at the time, coming home from Uncle Masty's home) when I walked in there was Herbert, sitting at the table all smiles. He simply said;

'Hello Mick' and as I hadn't seen him for years I was lost for the moment, not recognizing who he was for a moment. He got up and I looked at Auntie, sort of puzzled like.

'Don't you know who he is?'

I shook my head and shrugged my shoulders.

'That's your cousin Herbert, he just got in after all this time'

'Herbert' I said and he laughed and said;

'You take a it of recognising yourself Mick' and Kissed me.

'Grown hasn't he Mum. Do you still like bloaters Mick?'

I smiled and said yes.

'Well I've sent for some for you!'

Frank walked in with the shopping Auntie had sent him for and unwrapped 6 big bloaters! Gosh! What a feed we had eating them with our fingers. A lot of chatting and of past affairs. My wanting to go to sea cropped up and Herbert laughed and said that he would see if he could get me fixed up. It was a happy cheerful evening for all.

On Thursday it was pay off day for Herbert and he arranged to take me down to the shipping office at the Connaught. The 'Highland Pride' was paying off on that day too and Herbert introduced me to George Saxton, the Quartermaster of the Pride. Herbert, he and I went into the Connaught Arms which was crowded by those just paid off and called a round in, mine was a shandy. It was

arranged that George Saxton would put out some
feelers for a berth for me and would pop round
home when and if one was fixed up for me. To say
I was excited by this was to put it mildly. On the
Saturday, the 14th October, George Saxton (who
lived in Butchers Road Custom House No. 12),
came round and said to Herbert that I was to go to
his house and be there by 7.30 on Monday the 16th.
He would take me along to see the federation
delegate (The Sailors and Fireman's Union of
Seamen) who would see for himself the material I
was made of. Herbert was to stand reference and
security for me and George Saxton was to be my
sponsor (which shows how quickly destiny can
work). Uncles Stormy and Masty would also vouch
for my credentials too and it was arranged I should
go back with George to his place to be given a few
tips along with correct answers I must give to
questions asked of me. Herbert was tickled by all
this and poor Auntie was on the verge of tears
(whether they were of joy or fear I never knew). It
was also arranged that we were to go to Uncle
Stormy on the Sunday and tell him the programme.
I went with George to No. 12 and he gave me the
'gen' on the set up for Monday. Monday couldn't
come quick enough for me. When Uncle Stormy
head about it he sat me on his knee and patted me
with the joy of it.'Its what you wanted son, isn't it?
It was all so exciting, and with his

    'We'll keep our fingers crossed for you' it was
arranged that he and Masty would be at the

shipping office in case they be needed. I can vividly recall the examining officers words after all the references were given, they were:

'It's not so much the talk that counts, it is what he will turn out to be that matters!'

He stamped a 'Board of Trade Passed' on the signing paper, giving one copy to Herbert, one to the delegate and one for us all to sign, all in clear small print. I was eligible now to sign on any sea going ships of the mercantile marine (the first steps of getting my blue book), which George Saxton took to get me a berth on the H&W Nelsons Highland Pride. I had nine days to go now, to be called off, i.e.; to report on Monday 23rd as we were to sail on Tuesday 24th (there were two sailings a week, Tuesdays and Fridays). Another visit to the Counaught Arms for a celebration and we, or they, rolled merrily home well satisfied with the days events (I stood my 'round' like an old hand, amid 'Cheers, Good Health and Good Lucks') Auntie hugged and kissed me, even Frank did too when the news broke. 78 was a full house that Monday night. The question of suitable gear cropped up, George had control of this and was to see to it I was rigged out for it. He had explained what a 'Galley boy' should take on his first trip, giving me the tip to take a couple of potato peelers with me (thruppence each then) because one of my main day jobs was to prepare vegetables and peel lots of potatoes and quickness was wanted. Ever since then I've always had one by me, even in the army and how so handy a tool to have. I still have one now, a small knife and honing stone to keep it sharp. I think the lot of gear (including bed) came to two pounds and ten shillings, and with my other bits and pieces saw me kitted out. George gave me a jersey with HW Nelsons house flag and although it was miles to big for me it saved the cost of a new one and it gave me prestige when I wore it. I went to No. 12 each of the waiting days and George took me on board and showed me round, introduced me to the hands. By the time of signing on I was established near enough and a last the 29th came around. Signing n and calling off was to be at 10 o'clock so I had better tell you how this was done. The shipping office (it's still there as it was then) was situated on the corner of Connaught Road and Victoria Dock Road, a big Victorian red bricked building of the Board of Trade, a magnificent place. To enter it was by and through two swing iron trellis gates (fastened back when open) along a walk of blue bricks and red. On the right hand side would be standing 'hands' waiting or looking at the blackboard whereon would be the names of ships which were do to call off and sign on (another, the afternoon board, had those due to pay off). At the end of the walk, down some steps and into the waiting bay, one side of which was a canopied shelter with seats along it, about 20 feet in length, which gave access to two swing doors which allowed entrance to the 'Call off' room, bare of everything (and has seen some fights and melees as men fought each other to get a berth). At the far end was a raised dais with a barrier counter for Ships Officers to call off crews. On the side was an adjoining room into which men called off would enter to sign on, to get their half note (half a months salary to bond and bind them, to help them buy their gear for the trip). When the officer 'Called', the keen eyed experienced officer, who had long dealings with crews and could weigh his men up with one quick look, took the crews book, looked at it and either kept it, which meant you were on, or gave it back to the chappie. Returning the book didn't happen very often, but when it did that man was finished for good unless he signed on a Jonah ship, I was to see it happen only twice). I think it was the name of the previous ship that was the clue to those keen eyes. When you went into the room there would be a long table and your book would come in, your name called and you signed the 'Ships Articles'. You then turned left to get outside into the bay again. The door only opened outwards and a warder like chap in 'B.O.T square rig' (sic) saw you out and nobody from outside could possibly enter to work a 'double shuffle'. Once outside with the half note you walked up the steps where a Chappie would cash it (one shilling and sixpence commission) and opposite him would be the Union delegate to collect his subs (another five shillings, or whatever you owed). Invariably many of those who signed on would be in the Connaught Arms for a livener or a celebration.

Those that didn't get signed off would walk defeatedly (sic) out (I was to experience this in time to come when, for love nor money, was a berth to be had) to await the next sign on. With George as my sponsor it was just a matter of walking in and through that door and sign, I was in and out in seconds. I was Galley Hand 2nd Class at four pounds ten shillings a month for 2 months duration of trips to Monte Video and Buenos Aires – the Argentine Run'. I felt ten feet tall that day, everything had gone smoothly and I arranged to meet George at 4pm when he finished work. I went home and had a steak and kidney putting and suet duff afterwards. I met George at the steps of the custom house and went home with him, fixing up for the morrow, cartage for our gear and beds to be picked up at 11am to be on board by midday. Sailing time was 4 bells (2 o'clock). Do you know, I couldn't sleep that list night at home. I was up at 7.30 all itchy to be going. Poor old Frank, he was visibly upset, Auntie was too but Herbert, well, he was all smiles. Hectors van was at the door at 9 o'clock, collected by bits and bed and by 10am I was on my way to Nr. 12 and was there by 10.45. A quick cup of tea later and we set out to 'tram it' down to the steps, up and over them and at the end of the railway bridge there was our boat, ready to welcome us aboard! It was a bustling scene, the last moments before casting off, the Port of London Authority tugs were fore and aft, steam spewing from funnels, waiting for the signal of the Harbour

Master, showing the right of way (3 black balls showing clearance). We stowed our gear which was already by the 'focsal waiting for us. We started getting settled in, our names had been marked off as being aboard by the Officer of the Watch as we came aboard, George going to his deck cabin with a casual; 'See you Mick' and I went below to my berth bunk and made myself busy for I had to be at the galley for 4 bells (2'oclock) for evening duties (washing up and cleaning Dixie pots and pans and getting the next days odds and ends into line). I was kept busy 'till 8 bells (4 o'clock), 'till evening meal (Officers dinner at 6 bells so I had an hour to myself to have a bit to eat). That is when, having cleared the lock gates and tidal basin, we were underway under our own steerage. I sat on the Poop and in the fading October mists saw my London getting lost in the mist and smoke. I still hadn't got over the spell and speed of it all yet, if it hadn't been for the noise of the screws and the shaking of the vibrations I would have thought I was in a dream. I heard 5 bells go as we passed Erith Rands Point and close by were the Arethues and Cornwall on our port side. Can you imagine how I felt as I saw them as we slid by. There was no need now to hide and I stood by the Poop rail and watched them until they were out of sight as we passed Purfleet point. Yes, there was a red and white point light glowing as I'd seen it so often before. Soon we would be in Gravesend Reach then Long Reach and Sheerness on our Starboard bow. But needs must and I was due for the galley station and I couldn't be late for that! I was glad I had my jersey on, I put it on for it was getting kind of chilly now. I was soon busy again doing my last 'trick' of the day, washing up pots and pans and stowing them away in their racks. When I say 'pots and pans' they were big heavy copper ones which moved and rolled around with the ship, something I had to get used to! We passed Dover and the Isle of Wight, with its flashing light house at The Needles, and being in 'ballast' we were rolled around a bit. I was told;

'Alright son, off you go', I knocked on Georges cabin door and heard his;

'Come in whoever you are, oh, its you Mick, how did you get on?'

'Alright I think' and he laughed, telling me that he was sure I would in time. 8 bells went, which was supper time which I shared with George. I cleared up and said;

'Good night George' and he told me;

'From now on son I'm 'Quarter', it is the recognised term on board, 'Quarter', got it Mick?' and I replied, smiling and saluting;

'Yes Quarter!'

'Goodnight Mick, see you tomorrow'
I hadn't been below to quarters since Victoria Docks, and my appearance in my jersey caused an uplift of brows.

'Hello son, where you been? Thought you had fallen overboard'

I explained Id been working in the galley and sitting on the Poop deck and a voice said;

'I wondered who it was up there'.

One of them offered me a mug of coffee which I thanked him for and that started what I shall call the 'pedigree' questions.

'Who are you?'

'Where are you from?'

'First trip eh?'

'Hey Tom, here's your new mate!'

'I know, I met him earlier'

Tom was 18 and had done 7 trips aboard the Pride I was to learn. We liked each other from the beginning and got on like a house on fire. He taught me quite a lot actually, I loaned him one of my many 'spud peelers' and eventually gave it to him as a keepsake. I was his friend for life after that! He was a cook 2nd class and many the tid bits he gave me. I was tired by this time and was probably still in a daze because of all that had happened, the rebound was yet to set in! I would like to explain the impression, through a lads eyes and his feelings, of his being, for the first time in a Foc'sal, with strange men with whom I was to live, eat with and work with. When a days slog was done, of the leisure, off hours of what I learnt. The meaning of monotony and of the grave. One can, if one may be allowed, to get into the living conditions of those quarters and the hobbies of the crew, of the sea code of these men. Of seeing new and foreign parts, which to a lad was life opening up its secrets. Of how it sharpens the mind and enlarges its philosophy and the different feelings one has acquired too. Long shore living, of coming home and the eagerness to be home again and when you do get there the dissatisfaction with the stillness of the days ashore. Ever wanting to be off again and never being really settled. I shall attempt to do this in the next part. As I said, it could be a long story so I ask, if I am being boring, be patient with me and as I turn in for the night in my bunk.

I remain lovingly,
Dad

Chapter Ten

A lad who got by
Part two

As I am writing from memory and not having the means or assistance of a diary to go back into the mists of time some 57 or 58 years, several points are bound to be overlooked and not being a trained writer I must be excused if at the time of writing this happens. It is not an 'hour by hour' nor a 'day by day' chronicle of events but rather a 'here and there' record. In any case, the picture I wish to draw will give the reader some of the salient facts and must be accepted as I state them in this 'cyclopic' (sic) effort. What may seem to be leader points are only written to give some bone to my story and if the reader has some knowledge of sea life as it was in those war years the reader will be able to relive again those years, keeping in mind the writer was a young and impressionable youth of first experiences and will make allowances for receptitude (or lack of it). First impressions can last, to remain forever and can be easily gone back over such as this story contains, for there is and never will be a writer who can give a minute by minute record of what was said, who to, when or where. Of their life, especially when it has been so varied as mine. But the reader will agree that there are not many slip ups in my narrative, any verbal discussions could be enlarged upon possibly? No part or sentence is conjectural, only as the mind recorded and the eyes saw them. So, on with my story, as it is only a record, nothing can be retracted or altered. Shipping commerce in the 19th and 20th Centuries was a controlled system and the lines and companies were controlled with an iron rule. The Customs and Excise, Board of Trade and Lloyds Insurance were the big three and one would have to read volumes of these books on the Mercantile Marine since circa 1725-1974 (and only those who were really interested would be bothered to read them). It has come a long way, from Dhows and Clippers and on the safety side stands to the credit of on Samuel Plimsoll (1824-98) who, by his bill in 1876, made this a hard and fast law. His bust is on the north side of the Victoria Embankment by Victoria Gardens (Board of Trade) and the coast line around the British Isles are safeguarded by Trinity House which also controlled the tickets allocated to Ships Officers, after a severe and testing examination(s). the Mercantile traders are controlled by a searching scrutiny, the insurance by Lloyds who have brokers to safeguard the financial side. Two wars and German U Boat warfare was to change very drastically man of the shipping companies and only the names of a few are left after merging with the monied shipping companies. Several of those I knew are now extinct or absorbed into nonentity and H&W Nelson Shipping Line is one of them. The Highland Clan, NZSC, and Elder-Fife were the 'Fridge' ships, built for the purpose of carrying frozen meat trade from Australia, N.Z. the Argentine (River Plate) and Canada (Michigan) via the Lake Run (via Canadian Pacific Railway). The Clan Line served the route Clyde-Elder-Liverpool-Fyffe-Cardiff-Bristol. The Highland Line served London(Smithfield). These Fridge tubs were squat built, their holds were cold chambers, and were naturally ducks on the water, like floating corks, especially in ballast. The NZSC were semi-ducks too, roll, pitch, toss like a bucking bronco at the slightest sign of a sea running and this was my first trip on deep water! No, not the kindest way to break a new hand in and the first few days till we hit the 30 degree of latitude was I able to care or even tell what day it was. Oh dear, I was ill, and if there is a sickness like sea sickness and you have to somehow work through it, you tell me, because I don't know of any! I felt a bit headachy and queasy when I turned in. Now there is something about a Poop Foc'sal which, once encountered never forgotten. Dimensions of quarters were roughly 40 feet by 12 feet by 8 feet and into this is packed 42 bunks, one on top of the other in two tiers. A 6 feet by 2 foot 6 inch iron frame with side stops to save

being tossed out. It smells at all times like stale
tobacco smoke and white lead on turped paint. Its
ventilation by slots in the bulkhead and air being
taken out by luck really. Fresh air by means of the
entrance door. Imagine what it is like when 30
bodies are sleeping, eating and smoking in it (and
some of these said bodies suffering from BO). Or,
if after beans and onions a 'quiet one with slippers
on' is let go! Suffer all this in sea sickness and you
really want to die, truly! Cold, shivering, vomiting
ill and have to work on the lee side of the Galley,
peeling spuds and the odours of food cooking
wafting to you, and you are wishing why Did you
ever let yourself be conned into going to sea? I can
say one thing for it though, it certainly cleans ones
system out and one is not constipated afterwards.
George was very helpful, if not sympathetic. H
recommended I should drink some sea water from
the cock and keep drinking it 'till I stopped
vomiting, and the cow of a boat only rolled all the
more. All I wanted to do was curl up somewhere
warm and sleep but George said to work it off and
when I could get a break to go along to the
stokehold fiddle and bed down there 'till I got over
it. Next time I made my way aft I brought a blanket
up and snuggled down to it there. George, on the
side, must have told the ships cook and made it
right for me because I was not disturbed by anyone,
and lo, by Friday I was as right as a pudding,
except for feeling weak like. A feed of boiled rice
and curry and soup and I did my job as though

nothing had happened. Hitting the 30 degree line about Cape Finisterre it was a little calmer and the air warmer and each day saw me like a new boyo! I didn't go aft 'till midday Saturday and as I walked in those at the table got up and backed away in mock fear. 'Gawd, 'es come back!' two rushed and pushed past me and made for the door and I went to my bunk and it was bare, the paillasse was gone and so was my gear. I looked around and they were still at the end of the quarters. 'Where's my bed?' I asked (and not knowing what was going on, looked around me). 'Blimey, 'es alive, he just spoke! Where have you been cock, we thought you had gone over the side so we shared your gear out, but here have you been?' I told them and they came and sad down or relaxed in their bunks and they laughed then, belly shaking laughter and gave me my things back. 'We were only having fun Mick, are you feeling better?' I nodded and one gave me a mug of coffee and after that I was one of them, and what a bunch of good, rough, kind boyo's they were. I washed and turned in and by cross talking, answered their questions. The quarters, situated on the starboard side was the 'weather' side, but on the run home would be on the lee side. Built above the shaft tunnel, the noise of the screw (single turbine) was pretty noisy for, as she clipped, the screw would be partially out of the water and would shake the quarters, yet one got used to this after a while. I had a top bunk opposite the door and really it was the best bunk of them all for being opposite the door meant fresh air! Blowing the smoky air aft and it was hand, out of everyone's way. I was to have this for my two trips on her. I was told it was the first trippers privilege, and the bottom one was toms. Each watch shared the 10 man (5 each side) forms at the table and when off duty someone was always sitting there doing little hobbies or pastimes and having their meals (Tom and I had ours in the galley). We were coming off Cape St. Vincent (Lat 38N Long 10 west), the air, though still blustery was warmer and smoother (thank goodness) but being a force 4-6 was blowing on the star fore quarter causing her to dip, roll and throw a slucier (spumes/spray) and as the sun caught the edges would cause a rainbow effect, very pretty this with cumulus cloud and the white crests against the glass green of the sea. It was fascinating to see and all I had to do was look out of the porthole by my head to see, involuntarily flinching back when a big sea splayed against it. I was lulled to sleep and really enjoyed my first good nights sleep. The morning came with a wakening mug of warm coffee (no milk) but real ships freshly ground coffee, it is something to really taste and enjoy. Very rarely was tea ever dished up and I missed it at first (I was tipped off to have some saccharin tablets to supplement the sweetening of it and right handy they were to turn out to be). We were due for Tenerife soon, early next day, as I went up to the top boat deck to where the vegetables were stored I saw a school of Porpoises cavorting over and around the bows. We were doing a steady 10 knots and what a fascinating sight they were. We weren't far off from land for the gulls were still with us, flying just aft, diving into the sea to pick up, I suppose, fish, dipping, flanking diving what wonderful skilful flyers they are. But Mother Carey's chickens (the Storm Petrel) can beat them easily at this manoeuvre. Getting the days vegetables out of the locker cabin and down the chute was heavy and tricky at first, get the pails out and set to, preparing the veg for the day. My days started at 6 bells (7am) and at 8 bells had breakfast (and I was ready for it too). 20 minutes for breakfast and by 1 bell had my first 4 pails ready (bless that peeler). Cabbage, two net bags, Leeks and Onions, the time simply flew by (Tom would be doing the Tomatoes and chopping the Onions) and by 5 bells porridge and coffee and odds and pieces to do in a big wooden sink. Dry these and stack away above my head in a rack and by 7 bells be clear! I would have a break and find some little thing to clean with brickdust and soda water or, if Chief of the 2nd Officer wanted anything special done a call with instructions saw me at it. Dinner for Officers and Passengers 1st class was served a 6 bells (7pm) but midday was crew time and at 1 bell (12.30) their 'Peggy's' of the mess would be there at 12.15 collect and away aft and so these pots and pans again. A break for us galley staff and having that, prepare for afternoon and evening meals. No dears, we had no idle time except breaks of a few minutes and we were always kept busy. The staff had their respective watches (12-4 4-8 8-12). The earlies, then middle watch (12-4) were the bakers and 4-8 the breakfasts and 8-12 the lunch and dinners. We broke (or not mine and Toms) watches into the opposite. Deck crews watches of 'Dogs' (12-2 and 2-4 early mornings) and we had ours in the afternoons. Mine and Toms were 4-6pm (4 bells) were pots and pans etc again, 'till 1 bell (8.30pm) and when a day was finished we were ready to bunk down. But of this we didn't mind, for it meant we had some of the evening free and all of the night in bed (best job time on ship!) We arrived at Tenerife and laid off shore for an hour or so, picked up a pilot who laid us along side the jetty pier. Some passengers and ships officers went ashore and we off loaded some crates and took on fresh vegetables, tomatoes, fruit and water. No one was allowed ashore and we stayed about 14 hours before we cast off and were soon at sea again. Tenerife, what little I know of it (and I expect it has all altered now) was of snow white Haciendas and mostly Spanish customed (sic) and still something 17th century about it. Slow, calm, steady, stately even the Peons or Labourers were gentlemanly in behaviour. Polite, smiling, gleaming white toothed, all very 'apple pie' I liked it really! We were on a straight run now for the Plate and making good time in fair weather. The early westerners were yet to blow and in a rolling sea we hit the Plate Lightship about 6 miles out, leaving it on our starboard beam. In an hour or so we'd be berthed. Tom had told me tales of the place and of Monte Verde and Buenos Aires, to go into detail would take pages and a far better pen than mine to describe. I dislike the place okay, okay? Like all places, first times, first impressions stay and when the novelty of being there had worn off I disliked it or rather, felt disappointed with it. Perhaps, as I thought of Toms tales, I might see it differently, as his eyes did, but his taste and choice were different to mine. Was it the haze of the place, its smells, its general lay out or perhaps its people. Was it this, along with the lowing of the long horns (soon to be hung in our fridge)? Was it the manner of the supercilious wine drinking consignors and their lingo and both these two towns have their fair share of them, what was it I disliked so immensely? (I took the same dislike to Bristol and some parts of the Irish district of Liverpool too!) This may seem strange to you the reader, so this was the famous Plate – Ugh! You can stick it.

The second trip there I was to show it, I still have the 4 big scars on my hands to show and remind me of one 'Signor' who pulled a knife on me. I made him drink the blood of a 'Gringo' and stamped him into the sidewalk planks and showed his pals that an Englishman fights with his hands. I couldn't peel a banana let alone vegetables when I got back on board (or rather, was carried by for of the crew to the sick bay for repairs to my hands and arm). The Captain held his enquiry over it and it upset his balance of calm as the police asked what was going to happen of the bloke I had left packaged on the quayside. The crew and Tom who was there explained and a couple of ladies spoke in my favour, saying the 'Vaqueros' was a 'Toro' and had everyone in fear of him. They also said I was a brave boy not to be frightened of him. I got barred from going ashore or even coming on deck! Word had gone around that I was 'El Locos', a crazy man if let loose! But I will bet you this, I stopped his knife pulling once and for all or at least he'll think twice on doing it in the future, wanna bet?. One of the officers, 2nd mate Mr. Jackson said I'd done a silly thing and the Skipper said he had done the sillier thing to let this chappie (me) do what he was accustomed to doing. But the crew liked the way I'd done it because a little more respect was show to the 'Gringo's' after that (or at least the crew of the 'Pride' were). I will tell you of this incident in detail a little later. Those days in Buenos Aries were busy loading days and at last, battened down and decks cleared with a tug on tow to take us out into clear steerage we were off again and it was good to get out into the clean fresh sea air again. Now I know and I am pleased that we get no more beef from there (the ban was caused by the foot and mouth diseased meat which caused such an uproar over here in the 20's and has been in force ever since). Those 'Mexi's' have not the slightest feeling for animals, or humans come to that, I don't like them at all. We were deep in the water with tons of carcasses aboard and dropped to 8 knots as we sailed for the Canaries again or Madeira to pick up deck cargoes of oranges and nuts for the Christmas trade (you can bet some of these were to be broached into the ships store for future use. We had 3 days in Recife (Brazil) for Oranges and nuts and fresh water and coal and had fairish weather until we got to Cape St. Vincent area and ran into a 'seven winder', known as a round the clock force 10, a real 'hell blower' which was a real up and downer. We took a list to starboard and sailed lop sided for 8 days, fighting every inch of the way 'till we reached Ushant just off the French coast, then and only then could we steer a North by East to the Scilly Isles so as to get through the 'Narrows', a tricky part of the Channel. (Remember the Torrey canyon affair?). We could see the Eddystone light, like a big searching finger, every 8 seconds, swing from East to West. In a day and a half we would be in the Albert Dock again, to sleep in a steady bed once again and even at that point the crew were tidying and collecting their bits in readiness. All eager, after 16 weeks, to be home again once more. We slowed at the Narrows to pick up the Trinity House Deep Sea Pilot and slowed of Plymouth to try and shift some of the cargoes to straighten up the beam again. Everyone helping, we deck crew the deck cargo and some down the hatches with the meat. It was the cases of Armour Hams, big jobs, that had broken loose and moved

139

which had caused the list. Needless to say some of these were put by to supplement the diet on the next trip over! We were home on the 22nd December and paid off on the 23rd and had Christmas at home!

What a welcome I got, to a full house. Auntie Mill, Polly, Masty, Stormy and Arthur were there! Kisses all round and comments as to how well I looked. The baby of the family had finally made it! I had brought some presents home. Silk shawls and lacework and a pretty colour woven basket and pieces of brown and red pottery. Kisses for these and lots of 'He's a good boy' etc. I spent the night telling them little snatches of stories, of my sea sickness spell amid 'Poor little soul' and 'will you be going again? When? Will you stick it? It isn't too hard is it? Frank smiling in his quiet way and his asthmatic coughing chuckle. He was proud of me, genuinely so. So a good time was had by all. It was agreed, before I'd gone ashore that my berth was open for me for the next trip and this had been arranged. As George and I had come aboard together, we went ashore together, to his place first and then to mine. Mrs. Saxton, a very homely woman, gave us a lovely welcome and she gave me my first 'Best cup in the house' cup of tea and Scotch cookies and buttered toast. I thanked her for these and gave her a string of sea shell beads I'd bought for her in Recife. She hugged and kissed me for it and asked me to put it on her neck and two teas came in her eyes as I did so. She was all ears as George gave his report on me and kept her eyes on me all the time and said 'Wish I had a son like him'. George laughed and said to me 'Hear that Mick, you are honoured!' I stayed for dinner with them and George took me home to 78, to Auntie and Frank. He said he would see me at the shipping office at 10am and see that everything was in order because he had to hand me over and reclaim his £5 bond. He cleared the papers for me and we had a drink in the Connaught Arms saying our 'cheerios' to my crew mates. We were to sign on again on a date that we would be told of by letter. The next fortnight seemed to fly by. I had been paid off with £6.10s of which I gave £6 to Auntie. Settling down to wait we had a jolly Christmas and on Boxing day went over to Auntie Milly and it was arranged that the following Sunday we would all go to see Mum. I had bought a beautiful shawl for her and when Mum saw it and put it round her shoulders (which I did for her) she cried, holding me tightly. I did too, in fact all 6 of us did until the nurse came up and told us not to upset Mum anymore as they had to deal with her after we had left. To cheer Mum up I gave her the pearl inlaid snuff box and a pound tin of S.P. snuff, which she loved. (Women didn't smoke then but used snuff). A pound of snuff would last her out until I came again and she still had some left from my last visit to her. This really cheered her and she kissed me again and again, feasting her eyes on me. Those two hours

with her went like minutes. I still can see her
waving as I went away wishing I could take her
back with me (but Mums proudest moment of her
life was when I turned up in my Navy Uniform, I'll
never forget that day ever!). It all seemed so
strange to be home again, in the room, so quiet, a
little coal fire and gas light. Yet there was a sort of
hemmed in 'hutch like' feeling about it but after the
cabin on the stumpy barge 'Hornet' (and how small
a quarters can you get than that – you tell me), 78
was 6 times larger and that sort of compensated.
But after the 'Prides' quarters, with its lively
boyo's and activity it seemed a different world. I
missed it somehow, to be able to sleep in peace was
not appreciated then and I wanted to be back
aboard. The waiting days seemed a waste of time, I
missed the odours and smells of the galley and life
seemed to be slipping me by and I, in my
impatience, had to wait. Such is a wanderer made
of – restlessness. The next couple of days were
spent sorting out my things. Frank made mention of
sewing gear and we started chatting over this. He
gave me a version of how he spend some of his off
watch hours making mats from Manila Hemp
ropes, how they were done and what needles to use.
He told me how to keep the needles in an oilskin
wrapper inside a small pencil box (a habit I never
ever let go of and I still have by me my needles, of
all sorts, in a pencil box – to had for whenever
needed). Give me a line, and I'll make you a
doormat or table mat even now! So, when next

time we went out to stock up these articles would be laid in ready, also little essentials, which I did not have on my first trip. Frank enjoyed these 'laying in shopping' days because it reminded him of his time. He knew many angles, where to go and how much to pay and so my £2 went a long way. Things were cheap then, we spent many happy hours foraging around the chandlers stores. In these stores you could buy anything from a needle to a haystack and I was well equipped for the future. I even had my own sea chest (12/6d) in my room. I could neither read nor write but that didn't bother me (not then).

We three (Frank, Auntie and I) would go to the Bioscope (cinema) twice a week, Auntie enjoyed this outing and in the 3d seats at the matinees (afternoon shows) you were given a cup of tea and three biscuits in the interval. On the Saturday we went to the Imperial Palace Music Hall, front stalls (6d) and 1d for the programme and to have a good night out a 'Fish and Tater' supper afterwards (3-9d). So, for 2/6d a most enjoyable night.

During the week I took Frank to see the 'Pride' and felt very proud doing it. We saw George and had tea in his cabin and went to No. 12 with him. Ma made a fuss over us, she kept a nice home and was homely and kind. Like Auntie she saved a penny or two for a 'rainy day' (and she, like many others, were to need it in a year or so when the ships were hard to get). Even though George had been with Nelsons since a 1st tripper like me, he got the knock in the end, in 1922. I think this broke him up and when I saw him in '27 he didn't look the same man! By this time Ma had gone white haired but was still a loving soul. Such is how life treats you. I will not dwell on this any further except to say that in 1927 she was still wearing 'my' necklace and with tears in her eyes she smilingly said to me 'See, I've still got it Mick'. When I left I gave her a couple of pounds. What a sorrowful parting to what was a happy start for me many years before.

Over the years I've often thought of them. So, we come and go, out of and back into the mists like ghosts. On Friday 19th January (1917) I had a letter telling me the signing on day was to be the 22nd January (Monday) and would I report at 10am on that date etc. The weekend was a round of goodbyes to uncles and Aunties in Poplar and getting ready for Tuesday. Duly signing on on Monday, straight in and straight out, £2.10 the richer, my wages had been risen a £1.0.0d a month more and this I put in my blow belt as spending capital. I had nothing to buy as I did on my first trip. Auntie advised me to have a couple of pounds out of the bank in case I should need it. As I always listened to her advice I did so but I have always been careful with the coppers. It was comforting to know that I need never be short of a bit of what it takes to buy it when you want it (a good maxim this). Save a 3rd, spend a 3rd and give a 3rd away is one of my strong points even now, and a little saving never hurt anybody! Tuesday dawned and the van came for my gear at 8.30 and by 9.00 I was off, Frank coming with me. Auntie was in tears bless her and with her 'Take care Mick' I waved to her as we turned the corner. Leaving home an hour early could be very handy, it gave me a chance to get settled in before we cast off and believe me it soon goes. Saying and kissing Frank goodbye on the quay I boarded and reported in. Making my way aft, saying hello to the boys in the galley, on down to the well deck, waved to Frank one more time and went into the quarters. My gear hadn't arrived yet so I want back up to the galley to see if I could help. I was told not yet and to report back at 8 bells (12 noon), but was thanked for looking in and told that there would be more than enough for me to do later! Nearly two hours to go and so I went aft again, the crew came on board, one by one and we chatted about our days ashore. One was better off in there, out of the way, because on deck at the last moment is a busy place indeed, getting last minute touches in, odd jobs done. The noise of the deck winches getting last minute bits and pieces aboard or putting on shore – it is Bedlam pure and simple. Shouting, scampering feet overhead, yet, for all the seemingly last minute chaos, there evolves the marvellous pattern of system.

Everything is timed to a precision and what seemed like a jumble of things becomes tidiness. One has to see this to believe, what a short while before was impossible to achieve becomes like a jigsaw pattern into orderliness and tidiness. A shout 'Gears here' and the winches hoist their nets, sagging with weight, up, over and laid gently, like a mother with a babe, upon the deck. Eager Stevedore hands, practiced at doing it, lay it alongside the ships rail, gentle like, as thought they were dealing with china or eggs and the crew sorting their marked gear, orderly and quietly, picked it up, no slinging or messing about with other chaps gear. This is why coming aboard an hour early paid a dividend. Imagine a hundred odd paillasses in a single pile and ours is somewhere in there. Imagine a system where the pile is sorted alphabetically and one can get at it without too much confusion. This is how it worked. The 'unloaders' put A's where A should be and so on, neat and tidy like. The dock workers are hard working men, bless 'em. They may swear and be rough and tough hard working men but they are kind, generous and honest, and that is not too high a praise for them. They had their code of honour, they were brothers, belonging to a brethren in their essential unity. Their history is well worth knowing of and one has to see the conditions of their life to realise. (Excuse me for 'going over the side for a moment but it all helps to fill in one of the small details of impressions on a lad and should be included in the story) . I think the sea teaches

one lessons in life which are never forgotten.
Having got my gear down and settled while there
was yet time to straighten out and have to hand the
things I'd need (one learns to use spare valuable
time to its full advantage) and so by 8 bells it was
as though I'd never been ashore. The smell of paint
and smog was strong and it was a treat to report to
Chief (I was hungry and a 'slip' meal would be the
ticket at the earliest chance) There were pots and
pans and trays to wash and clean and it was soon
done. Chief was pleased to see how so different it
was to my 1st time there. I knew where and what to
do without being told. This bit of fore thought got
me a nice big tasty chop dinner and gratitude all
round. Casting off at 4 bells took place, the little
Port of London Authority tugs fussing and pulling
to the lock gates. I was watching them as I sat
getting the evenings vegetables done. It was cold
but dry, an East wind was blowing and the air clear
for once. Come 6 bells we were underway, passing
Woolwich Point, turning into Erith Rands. Well,
there was no turning back now, my 2nd had begun
but this time I knew what to expect. It would be a
repetition of the 1st except this time, having an East
wind (or following wind as it was known) blowing
astern, we cruised down the Channel this time and
dropped our pilot at Bishops Rock. We steamed a
steady 10 knots but this time a couple of Destroyers
had joined us because Jerry was getting busy off
the Channel and the south Irish coast. They were
waiting for loaded packets which were homeward

bound and would pounce on them. The Destroyers were to pick up the convoy off the Bay of Biscay and take over from the escort of Mediterranean ships via Gibraltar. The following day (Wednesday) saw no sign of them, we were alone on our own and this time we were bound for Valparaiso (Florida) on the Eastern seaboard of the USA s it was a straight run across. The wind had changed due west and was running high by noon, dipping and lurching. I felt a bit queasy and a touch of a dull headache with comes with sea sickness, but remembering the salt water remedy I had dinner on that! It took a day or two to wear off but a few bowls of soup put some food inside me and was something to bring up easy like if I wanted. But, feeling cold (as sea sickness makes you) I told the boys where I'd be if I went missing amid much laughter from them. After work that's where I went, to the top of the boilers where it was warm and fairly steady (one learns and remembers). It was a fair enough run out, making it in 28 days, bearing SE by S. I did all my outside work on the port side to keep out of the spume and wind which she shipped day in and day out. We hit Valparaiso at 7 bells just as I was going on watch. We slowed to pick up the pilot about a mile out and at half speed approached the river just as the sun was coming up. What a pretty sight, I think it lives up to its name 'Garden Port'. It is a ver very pretty looking town, I fell in love with it from the moment I saw its pretty hacienda style houses, snow white

148

and peaceful amid a green background as we steamed round the bend in the river. It became prettier and prettier. It is a natural tidal port, laid out in squares, the boats in each section something like New York. The sheds, snow white, looked like a fairy picture. The people, of true Spanish stock were a bit supercilious, as though strangers like us were, well, just sailors. Yet, they were polite, courteous and really nice. Even the dock or jetty workers, willing, smiling and ever friendly. I'd love to have lived there. I was in love with it. Should I ever go on a world trip, that's one of the first places I would make aim for, but would I find it the same? We went ashore and had a look around, it was still back in the 13th century in places, slow, easy and rather lazy with siestas in the afternoon. There was some dancing at night and horse drawn buggies, the drivers with their big sombreros and shawls. I spent 30/- there on knick knacks, they were to polite to refuse the offers I made. We had three days there, watering, coaling, fresh stocks and melons and grapes. One of the boys asked me what I thought of the place and I said 'It makes you feel like jumping ship and going adrift'.

Oh, while I think of it, everyone had to have a visa, a kind of passport with your photo, particulars and thumb print in case you couldn't write your name – and these had to be shown and stamped at every port of call on every visit. It was in

Spanish/Mexican and English and I wish I still had it, but like lots of other things it got neglected and lost. Even the policeman in the street could ask you to show it. Later on, the Western run had another. I've an idea I left it among my papers and discharge books when I left everything in Kingston District after Mum died and I sold the home (contents) to a Mr. Pearce for 2/6. I'm sick at that thought now but it cannot now be remedied eh? Being a hoarder of sentimentality, I carried and kept them all those years in oilskin wraps. So, fancy that love, the foolish things we do when distraught. All that I was left with was a change of underclothes and Enid's bits. I always regret I never did return the case I'd borrowed from Mrs. Rempstone. I was not to go back there until you loves took me from Lynham, remember?

So, on with my story, I stayed on deck the whole time it took to leave that lovely place. We were bound for the Plate and made fair time, hugging the coastline. We hit Monte in the early morning and dropped anchor to await a berth. Ugh, hurry up and get out of it. Monte is the Passenger port and the unloading of crates etc. and not very interesting being much like Liverpool or Cardiff or Bristol to me. Being in those ports afterwards reminded me of it, its smoky skin smells and decay. It seemed to have a perpetual musty cloud about it. We stayed 3 days here and then n to Buenos to load and my encounter with the conquistador Vaqueros Chappie.

It happened like this, any debris or rubbish had to be taken ashore twice a day, down the companion way, a set of steps especially for that purpose and that purpose only. No one but the crew were to use it and it was stated in Spanish/Mexican, English and even in German, the word Verboten being added to the bottom. This job, which was an extra, had to be done before work was commenced. On lowering the fore and aft gangways for the workers to come aboard, and they were there, babbling, gesticulating, eager to get on board for they were piece workers, were up and on before the gangways were even made fast. Our one was rigged up and hoisted and our stack of rubbish was already to go over the side. Tom went first to see to the fresh vegetable collection and I followed behind with two buckets. On getting within a step or two of the quay this geezer pushes past Tom and I, with two buckets filled up what space there was on the gangway. Now, the merchant must have been behind time for he was an overseer and should have been the 1st one on board (but that wasn't my funeral, it was his). He tried to push past me and I let go of one of the buckets to keep my balance. The bucket clanged onto his bare feet (hard luck!) and he yipped as he went backwards. I helped him with a non too gentle shove like and arse over head he went. The peons around started to laugh and I busied myself with retrieving the bucket and contents (I should have hit him with one there and then, it would have saved a lot of trouble all round). Whether because of prestige or because of the laughter set him off who knows? Up he gets and out comes this shiv and I caught his action. I had heard of their fondness of using the blade. I turned to face him as he made a quick pass at me, missing the first time. I dropped the buckets and up went my hands, a natural defence, and I took the first slice on my middle finger of my left hand. The second slice ripped my little finger all the way down from tip to my palm. ZIP ZIP, as quick as that and I closed with him rather than go away from him and up he came, to rip my right wrist which was on its way to clout him. It all happened so quickly, close to him I tied his knifed hand close to my body, as he tried to get his hand clear. I, still going forward, he went backwards and how it happened I know not. I managed to grab that knife, I pulled and it came away and dropped. With my right hand I hit him full on and he just crumpled and buckled, I must have been blood mad. I was pouring like a stuck pig and my 'Paddy' was up. I bite like a terrier and he screamed. I kept biting his face, I was intent he should drink some of the 'Gringos' blood. I literally tore his mouth apart screaming 'Drink, drink you Dago bastard, drink!' With my knee is his testicles he was suffering. Before they pulled me off of him my last gesture was to stamp him there. Willing strong hands got me off of him, it was all over in a minute and I was taken aboard to sick bay. A tourniquet was applied to my wrist to stop the bleeding. A little more to the right and my ulnar artery would have gone, as it was it was only nicked. A little morphia was given to me for the pain. How long it took to restore order again and get gangs working I don't know, but they are an excitable race of guys but the excitement had died down. A couple of the ships officers came in to see how I was and when seen to I was sent aft and told to stay there. Later, they came back to get my version of events. Tom had seen it all and had said his piece, the gangway boys were there and I was cleared but told to stay where I was with a couple of my chums to stand by. I had got a 'dab' between my eyes and that swelled my eyes up and could feel the pulse of every heartbeat, throb, throb, throb as I lay on my bunk. One of them gave me a cup of freshly made coffee and I was all of a tremble, the reaction had set in. The morphia I was given was taking effect and I went to sleep. It was early morning, when the 1st dog watch came in that I remember next. I stirred and one came over and looked at me and gave me a mug of sweet coffee and asked how I was feeling. Now, I'm not partial to coffee and rarely have one now but when I do it stirs up memories of that one I had on coming round. It was the nicest drink I've ever had. I was dry and feverish and later on the sickbay attendant came to see me and I was shifted to the sickbay amidships. He gave me a whitish chalkish drink and I was soon asleep again. I stayed there 'til we left port a week later. No one except George was allowed near me. He was visibly concerned over me. I had been stitched up on my wrist with two tubes leading from it to take the surplus pus away. A lot of the ache had gone but being bandaged up as my hands were, and with swollen blackened eyes, I couldn't even hold the bottle which the sickbay attendant did for me. Each day saw me mending and on the 3rd day was allowed on deck for a spell and George asked that I be bunked down in his cabin. It was he, who going back over the affair said of the pitiful mess I'd left behind on the quay. Tom was to add to this part, having been an eye witness to all and it was Georges job as Quartermaster was also called afterwards. So, this is the way the Jennings went to work eh? Something like the crews fighting each other and his remark 'Bet he wont start ever again something he can't handle'. Bit of a Tartar when you're put out Mick eh? Handy chap to have around in a scrap' etc. A week out and I wanted to be doing some graft but my hands were too bad for that yet, but a new pair of 'elbow' rubber gloves got me into circulation again and I felt that I was earning my 'corn'. I had to go before the Skipper to listen with the others who gave evidence (on oath!) and he put it down in his log book under 'Incidents'. I was exonerated from any blame (that notice cleared me). There was nothing they could do about the knife carrying part as was a part of his trade to carry one. The Skipper had been ashore to report to the Ships Agents and Consul in case of further developments etc. but it all died down eventually. I stayed in George's cabin for the remainder of the trip and had to report to the Seaman's Hospital for treatment afterwards. I was glad I had bought all those knick knacks in Valparaiso because I wasn't allowed out of my quarters while in port in Tenerife. George, at my request, bought a present for Ma which cost £2.10/- (a lot of money). It was a glass cut dressing table set which glittered with brilliance. I got a big hug, like one you would give a son, and a long loving kiss from Ma who couldn't take her eyes off of it. If I'd given George a £1,000 he couldn't have been a happier man to see his 'Pet Love' (as he called her) look so happy. It was still there as she took me up to their bedroom in 1927, bless her. On our return we were paid off and as my hands and wrist were to take a bit longer to heal I missed my next signing on for the Pride and dropped out of circulation. At the end of March she sailed again and I was on the 'Stones' (unemployed) 'till the end of April.

Chapter Eleven

War Service

At that time a call was being made for volunteers for the Mercantile Marine Reserves (like the Royal Naval Volunteer Reserve) to man minesweepers on the West Coast and ship trade routes from Fishguard to Clyde. Employment was under Naval Articles and Rules but of Civilian Statutes, with special pay of £16.10/- a month 'danger money' etc. Now, that is money and money talks! I chatted with Frank and Auntie and the Uncles and I eventually signed up for the duration of the war. My 'book' was my passport and security, these were handed over, duly receipted and I was posted to H.M.S. Eagle depot Ship in Salthouse Dock, Liverpool. Medically passed fit I was kitted out with full navy gear with the rating of 'Stoker 2nd Class, all this was excitement for me, I lapped it up. It was like being back on the Cornwall again, with the same environment, smells, food that I knew so well, but instead of being confined to ship, I would be posted to a mine sweeper which was then in Canning

Dock awaiting crewing up. This was a new world, to go to sea with a lads dream of adventure. These little mine sweepers were dinky craft, which swept the Channel ways clear of mines that had been laid. I was to know Liverpool, of the Merseyside of the Mersey down to the Bar Lightship, Holyhead, Carnarvon Bay, Cardigan Bay, Fishguard back up to Blackpool to the Clyde, over to the Giants Causeway, Belfast, Dublin, Cork, across to Fishguard, over to the Isle of Man, back into Canning Dock, a round trip of ten days and then five days in port. Imagine dropping anchor every night in a different place along the coast. All night in your hammock, a lords life! Imagine my surprise on one morning, anchored away to Part was the Belle Boat paddle steamer, which, in peace time took day trippers from Tower Pier to Southend, Ramsgate, Margate to Clacton Walton, South wold Lowestoft and Yarmouth. I couldn't believe my eyes what I saw. We were a County Class navy built mine sweeper. I was on the Banbury, there were four of us (mine sweepers), there being two on sweep at all times with two Belle boats making a foursome of a sweep team. It was a holiday really for I never saw a single mine in the nine months I was on it. If the weather was too bad we'd not o out but lay hove to until it cleared. No wonder we were called 'Mother Murphy's Regrets' or 'Smooth Water Sailors'. But the worst was to come as we were, or at least some of us, recalled to the Eagle, given 14 days leave and were transferred to the

Western Fleet in Armed Cruiser boats of the
Ellermans Line which had been converted into
'Guard ships' armed with two quick firers on the
bridge, six 6inch guns with depth charges and a 4.7
gun on the Poop, pretty formidable eh? Always
light loaded we would roll like a cork. Each convoy
had 4 of these on 'Quarter Point' keeping their
flock inside them (To get some idea of this, read
'The Cruel Sea', it gives a real pen picture of the
set up). The only difference then and the 2nd war
was there were no 'Packs of Wolves' U boats so it
was fairly safe convoying, or was it? Read my
'Story of Fear' of just missing one meant for us.
The City of London was a passenger boat of the
Colombo-Bombay trade belonging to Ellemans
City Line. A German owned company impounded
for being German and used at Gallipoli for troop
movements etc. But, it had to be this 'Joker' that
they made into an armed cruiser. Our trips were St.
Johns, River St. Lawrence, down the coast to New
York and pick up the convoy and escort them over.
The convoy was bringing hams and food from
Montreal via Chicago home to England. The City
of London simply ate coal! What a hard cow to
satisfy, but we 'Trimmers' were lucky really, we
had barrows to get our coal in. On the old scale, it
was got by filing baskets to feed the fires, what
were the conditions for those poor sods, it doesn't
bear to dwell on it. She was a 16 fire job on two
marine twin boilers, fore and aft (8 port and 8
starboard). She wasn't built for the Western Run

with its 40 feet high seas and a nigh constant force 8-10 wind, bow on! Could she roll? She loved it, a 'Dirty' ship for even a moderate force 5 or 6 and get one of those North Westers blowing and you really knew you were at sea. Most of the 'Black Crowd' (stokers) were Liverpudlians and real sods of 'Flankers' to sail with. Many had stoved in ribs, broken legs or arms which meant 6 hour watches. I was a Jonah on a Jonah ship! Twice every trip she had to have her 'Smoke boxes' cleared and in part, descale the boilers. For £16.10/- we earned it plus, believe me! I did every trip in her and the last strew came when Armistice came, we did two more 6 week trips and finally came back round to Tilbury and I had to work on board while Port watch was on leave. It was December 24th, Christmas Eve and I asked for a pass to pop home for Christmas and was curtly told 'You will go when the others come back, got it?' Like hell! I was only a one and a half hour train ride from and it was Christmas, would you be tempted to flout Navy Articles or bite your nails and cry? Well, I was tempted and went adrift, AWOL and so had my Christmas fell off the City of London. My patriotism had gone out on the ebb tide and it stayed that way until the law came to No. 78 and took me with it. Escorted back to the Eagle. Now ironically renamed the Eaglet because of the new aircraft carrier being launched and duly christened HMS Eagle. The thought of a boat of her age, of her service since 1634 being made a 'chick' again tickled my fancy as I picked oakum in the same kind of cell as I did on the Cornwall. Life had turned a complete circle after all those years. I was due for my court and if the war lords could do that to the old Eagle, what would they do to me? I got 28 days in Walton jail and discharged in March 1919, losing all I had served for. Bounty, Medals, Honour, NO! I was given a 'Very Good' in my blue book and I got off with jam on it as I was given my back pay (£100) and an escort to Lime Street Station. I paid £2 for my ticket to London and settled for that. When I told Frank, Auntie and Uncles and Aunts there was much laughter over it .The finale of the story comes, had I waited just two more days I'd have been on my way home with 28 days leave pending discharge and all would have been 'Singapore and Sing Song' afterwards. So, just how much of a Jonah can you be after that? You tell me! The old mind boggles even now. But what is to be will be, all the tears and piety will not erase word of what is written. I was lucky to get a berth on the six week runs, getting fixed up on the ATL Line (Atlantic Transport Line) an American firm out of the Albert Dock to Baltimore Chesapeake Bay run as stoker at £20 per month. A lovely craft and god quarters, good food as only the Yanks know how. All electrically cooked nicely and served in a civilised manner. The only other line like this is the Canadian Pacific Railroad Line out of Liverpool and the Clyde. These are a real treasure trove, gold dust berths.

I am coming to the end of my story now, I could and may write of these two 'Lines' but I think that such a nice story does not fit in with this one. I was to be in the Army before the year was much older and into another world in my ever searching for something to settle in. Something that would pacify that restlessness, seeking for whatever lay over the horizon.

I have found it at last, in Stevenage in Pinewoods, what a lovely calm, scented name that sounds. All I have has turned out to be memories, but even in them I draw some comfort to say it has been worth it. I have no regrets, none whatsoever now. Even if there were, there is nothing I could do to alter it. So, adios lovers,
Lovingly
Dad

Reflections

Thank you for giving me a chance to open up
a safety valve and create from your few words
more pages of which I am hoping make interesting
reading. It has certainly given me a task to occupy
a few of these long silent hours, which went by far
too quickly. As I have stated, to roll the curtain
back and recall an era of time of some six and a
half decades past and pick up the highlights of
those years and bring them into focus again and
also keep them in as small as possible number of
words was a task. A task which I consider a
challenge well met! I have had to omit any
superficial items, and not add any superlatives to
my story. This is the sum object of essays, semi
memories sort of. The time element of recording
the composition of an essay being the art of being
concise. I am fortunate enough to have a retentive
memory because one does not learn a lesson the
hard way and then tend to forget it. Should I be
asked how past Victorian/Edwardian children spent
their leisure hours, well, this would result in a book
of several pages! Of an era of time when there were
five distinct classes or stations of folk who were

kept in their specific stations, very rarely moving or being allowed to move or elevate themselves from this Caste system. In those days one followed in fathers footsteps, women counted as nothing socially. A time when men were men and women kept their own duties and minded their own business. Children were obedient and were taught to be seen and not head. Even in children there was a caste system applied at that time. A season for everything a child did to play at, in their games, according to station in the social scale of their parents. The reader must necessarily remember that the Commandment '6 days shall thou labour, the seventh keep holy'. No matter to which class you belonged this was strictly adhered to, if not entirely obeyed. Sunday was Sunday, the only shops open were the Jewish shops, their Sabbath (the word means Day of Rest) was on a Saturday and even then, unless they were strictly kosher did they close because it is not against the Jewish law to employ Gentile labour. So, this allowed them to use Christians to work for them. One could always tell if a 'Yid' was Kosher by his shop (on the side, the average Pawnshop was owned by a Jew) and on Saturdays and Mondays Pawnshops were the busiest ones.

In reality life never stopped still in those days, Sundays were, to us children, Chapel going days. No playing, no looking at comics or at Sundays News of the World, no making things. It was all about going to the Chapel and singing Hymns, Hymns and more Hymns. Holding each others hands to and from the Chapel. To be given a 'Bible text', a pretty little cord you brought home to proudly show mama which you were given in return for the farthing you reluctantly put into the collection box or on a plate (to make sure it could be seen!) Even here swizzing could take place in the form of a button or disk dropped in the collection box instead of cash! Some would even drop the plate or velvet bag in order to retrieve their reward, pretending to help retrieve the spilled coins. Yours truly had his honour and was never guilty of this offence. I was too scared of what God would do to me, let alone my Father if he ever found out I'd committed one little misdemeanour on my way to or in or on the way home again. Why? Because I truly believed that he would cut my tail off if I ever did bring disgrace on the family's name. The Jenningses were respected as far as Chapel and Sundays were concerned. Sundays we were dressed, boys and girls, in our best and the Lord help us if we got as much as a speck of dirt on our hands or clothes. We started all Sundays in our night clothes, by hopping out of bed and kneeling on the cold floor to thank the Lord for keeping us safe through the night. This was done under the supervision of one of the 'elders'. No mumbling, every word said in a plain clear childish voice ('Because if I can't hear it how do you expect the Lord to?'). Then it would be downstairs to have a quick sluice and upstairs again to get dressed. Then, on command, downstairs for breakfast, sitting perfectly still, no fidgeting. Dad would say grace, we would eat and then say grace once more and then into the usual 'clearing away' programme before going into the sitting room to await Chapel going time. The Church bell would be chiming, the old cracked tinny bell of the Chapel would 'ding clink' out its call 'Come to God. God loves you all. God is kind to one and all – Amen'. After Chapel it would be home again in time for dinner. More grace, eat a good mean, grace again, a kiss from each of us to Mama and a thank you to Papa. Until afternoon Sunday School we would listen to Kitty trying to read from the Bible to us, showing Horace and I the coloured pictures in her Bible. After Sunday School it was tea time and having cleared away Dad would get the Family Bible out. This was a real leather bound gold edged book with a big metal clasp on it and as it was opened it played a Hymn. Guess what, a sailors hymn "or those in peril on the sea" Dad, with his sonorous voice and welsh pronunciation in rising and falling tones peculiar to the Welsh, he would talk and I would sit, truly entranced by this. I loved it, every minute. We would each have our Sunday School hymn book and from this we sung hymns to the soft toned concertina (and Dad, at least to me, could make it talk). It had Mother of Pearl inlaid on it, its box had Dads GFW Jennings on it and the date 1871. The children never asked personal questions so I never found out the story about its history. Get Dad, Grand dad along with Uncles Stormy and Masty as a quartet and you would hear playing to thrill you. That old floor in 27 Croydon Road has been shook to its beam ends from the jigs and dances emanating from those glorious chords. To hear those 'Taffy's' singing was never to be forgotten. Mum could do her fair share of it too, in her lilting 'Iriosh' voice. Her favourite and one I recall;

> Top o' the morning Biddy
> McGrew
> Top o' the morning Biddy to
> you
> Sure, yer me darlin' girl
> Sure me heart is in a swell
> Sure as Ireland is yer home
> Yer've got a pretty name
> Top o' the morn, top o' the
> morning Biddy McGrew

To hear her quaint speech was, as Grand dad put it 'Sure, with you I hear the Angels sing' as he tried to imitate her brogue. Auntie Esther, Uncle Stormy's wife was of Scot/Irish extraction and her quaint brogue was something else never to forget. Auntie Em was a true born East end Cockney from the Isle of Dogs, Wapping and when she had a few inside her she'd liven up any funeral morgue up and how she could twirl! Those ample legs of hers and her accompanying clapping of those chubby hands would sound above all the rest of them, keeping time to the concertinas. As children we were packed off to bed at six sharp. At 4 bells that Dad would ring (I recall getting a 'sender' for daring to touch it once, it was taboo!). I was fascinated with this big bras bell that had S.B Caroline on its side (probably one of Dads craft, though I still suspect it was Uncle Masty's bell, or at least he had something to do with it because he was the one who kept it polished). Perhaps sometime I shall describe No. 27 to you, of the many knick knacks with adorned the parlour and sitting rooms and Dads 'cabin' with 'Master' written on a brass plate which was screwed to it. Dare say this layout would fill a page or two of my reflections. Snuggled in bed 'tween Kitty on one side and Horace on the other we would be lulled off by the faint music, the street gas lamp shedding it yellow glow into the room. Another Sunday would end.

As I stated before, we are not the masters of our own destiny and it is foolish to think that we are. All of the 'My, I and Me' stuff and the 'I've done this and I've been to such and such a place' is only because destiny decided it was to be so. Maybe I was daubed a Jonah by a superstitious sailor but to supersede that, I have been very lucky too. Very very lucky indeed! I was blessed by having:
(1) A strong constitution

(2) A strong mind

(3) A strong power to live as my parentswould have wanted me to

The constitution has taken a hiding over the years, the mind is just the same, obdurate and mulish. The power to know right from wrong is ever 'on watch', ever ready to reason. The other traits I will leave open for others to judge as they find me, that is their prerogative. The 'I's' are the product and tools of destiny, to use as required while for 'Me', well, I think I am just a vassal in the pattern of things. I realise that life can really go to quickly, that the very unfairness of it is that having learnt, we are not spared long enough to bring our learning to bear for the benefit of others. Life is like that because we are told: Man propose, god would never be able to dispose.. A Dante's 'FORTUNA JUVAT' don't you think? So it is the case of 'Ours not to rave and cuss, but to face facts squarely' and how easy it is to falsify the idea that we and we alone make our future. How easy it is to become lulled into the suckers vortex of our own creation. Because, 'pride going before a fall' and the 'little things sent to try us', and test us. Having become wiser for the tumbles and falls and disappointments of being conned, learn to accept that stupid egotism can and does get you into turbulent waters. For life, in its more serious vein, calls for a settling of the account and whether we wish to or not, answer for our actions. With cup in hand, tongue in cheek, become humble and subdued to a greater power than ourselves. But that, being a deep subject, I will not go into it here.

I am out of the race now, I had my run. I do not regret, the tears have all dried up now but of lessons learned I can ask, can I go to the top of the class now teacher?

I have no qualms to face Grand dad, Grand mama, Dad, my dear Mum my brother and sisters and uncle Stormy and others. The 'Chip off the old block', the 'Jonah' has arrived, kit and dunnage, Ahoy there!

You asked for, and you got, a memoir!

Notes

Note 1: Siblings

Ernest raised four children, Ronald (Ron), Joyce (Joy), Enid and a stepdaughter Kitty. He makes many references to Ron and Enid in his writings and the letters were all addressed to Joy.

Note 2: SS Carpentaria

SS Carpentaria was launched 1904 in Middlesborough and owned by the British India Steam Navigaion Company Limited of Calcutta. She was.just over 435 feet in length and a little over 53 feet inbeam. SS Carpentaria was a passenger and frieght carrying steamship which weighed 5,766 tons gross with an average cruise speed of 16.5 knots. Fitted with refrigerated holds for the movement of perishable goods. She was later used as a troop transporter during the Great War

Note 3: Workhouse Leytenstowe

A parish workhouse was set up by Walthamstow parish in 1726 in rented premises on Hoe Street. In 1730, a purpose-built workhouse was erected on an acre of Church Common purchased for £6. The building, a simple two-storey design with eight rooms accommodating 30-40 inmates, cost £343.12s.3d. It was enlarged in 1756, and again in 1779, and by the 1820s usually accommodated more than eighty.

A new West Ham Union workhouse was built in 1839-41 in Leyton. It was designed by Alfred Richard Mason and was based on a T-shaped main block, with lower wings to the rear creating two courtyards for the use of male and female inmates. The building was extended to provide additional accommodation in 1845

The main block was a three-storey structure containing offices, infirm wards and a surgery on the ground floor, the Master and Matron's quarters and inmates' wards on the first floor, and lying-in infants' wards on the second floor. The rear wing contained a dining-room and stores and a kitchen in the basement.

Note 4: Seamen's Hospital Connaught

The Seamen's hospital Society founded the Albert Dock Seamen's Hospital in Alnwick Road Custom House in 1890as part of the Dreadnought Seamens's Hospital at Greenwich . It provided for the care of ex-members of the Merchant navy, the fishing fleets and their dependents. It remained open in that building until 1924.

Note 5: Goodmays asylum

Building of Goodmays Asylum commenced in August 1898 and was completed in August 1901. It as designed to accommodate up to 800 patients in two wings, one for men the other for women. It was for those paupers who were considered at the time to be mentally ill. The Asylum was further extended in 1908 with accommodation for a further 70 female patients. In 1918 the Asylum was renamed the West Ham Mental Hospital.

Note 6: Snaresbrook Hall

Snaresbrook Hall was officially named the Infant Orphan Asylum. It was opened in April of 1843. The object of the Asylum was to board, clothe and educate orphan children and those children of lunatics. Children were kept there until they reached the age of 14 or 15 and was able to accommodate up to 600. It was renamed the Royal

Wanstead School in 1938 and eventually closed in 1971. The building is now used as Snaresbrook Crown Court.

Note 7: TS Cornwall

Training Ship Cornwall was a fully rigged ship of the Black Prince Class although build according to the lines of the Vengeur Class. At almost 176 feet long and with a beam of almost 48 feet she weighed in at 1745 Tons. She was originally armed with a total of 74 guns including 32 pounder, 28 pounder and 12 pounder guns. Originally built in 1815 she became a training ship in 1860. TS Cornwall was certified for up to 260 boys. Boys were normally between the ages of 12 and 16 who were considered to be 'out of control'. Discipline was harsh and punishment routinely included the use of the birch. She remained on the Thames and was finally sunk during a bombing raid by the Luftwaffe in 1940 during the second world war. After the war she was raised, her figurehead removed and erected at the main gate of Chatham Dockyard using her original name of HMS Wellesley.

Note 8: Mount Edgecombe

In his writings of Mount Edgecome Ernest was actually referring to the Mount Edgcume which was originally commissioned as HMS Woolwich, a 56 gunner. In 1877 she was recommissioned as HMS Mount Edgcumbe as an industrial training ship for homeless and destitute boys. In many ways similar to TS Cornwall, the Mount Edgcumbe was eventually closed at the end of 1920, sold and taken to Plymouth for breaking up.

Printed in Great Britain
by Amazon.co.uk, Ltd.,
Marston Gate.